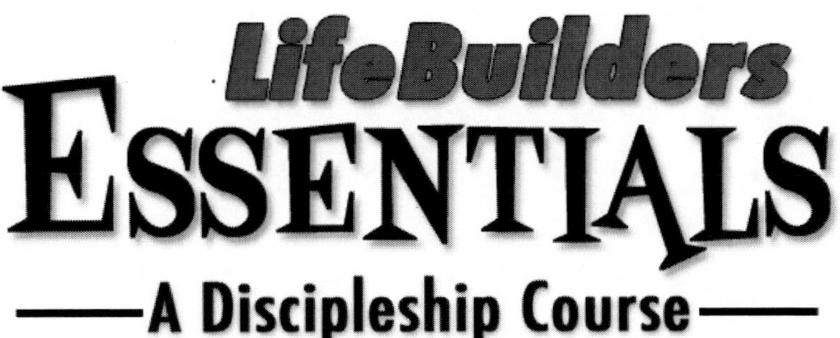

Twelve Steps To Becoming A Godly Man

Patrick Morley
Leonard Albert
Don Warrington

ISBN: 978-1-791725-55-6

Copies of this book can be ordered from:
Men's Discipleship International
P.O. Box 2430
Cleveland, TN 37320-2430

Telephone: 423-478-7286
Toll Free: 888-766-9009
Fax: 423-478-7288

E-mail: mensdiscipleship@churchofgod.org

Web site: http://www.lifebuilderscog.com

Introduction

Just before our Lord and Savior, Jesus Christ, ascended to heaven, He gave us the following command: "Therefore go and make disciples of all nations..." (Matthew 28:19). When we think of this Great Commission, we usually think of winning the lost. In a world where we casually talk about billions of people on the planet and trillions of dollars in the federal budget, it's easy to get caught in a numbers game, and too many of us look at fulfilling that Commission solely in those terms. When people talk about thousands and millions being saved around the world, we get excited, as we should.

But Jesus had more for the church than a long series of mass meetings and television ratings. His command was for us to make disciples because He knew that (a) a stable church is made up of stable people, well-grounded in His Word and rich in spiritual gifts, and (b) a stable church is the only platform from which we can hope to launch our efforts to win the lost and make our efforts stick for eternity. The experience of the New Testament church and the two millennia that followed have borne these truths out.

This is particularly true with men. Men are experts at hiding their innermost beings, but beneath the surface of work and sports, men desire a deeper walk with their Creator and with those around them. *LifeBuilders Essentials* is a 12-lesson course designed to bring that heartfelt desire to fruition and to give men a solid beginning in their walk with Jesus Christ, which will in turn affect the way they relate to their families, coworkers and the world at large. Ultimately the relationship they establish and cultivate with God will determine their eternal destiny, which is the most important thing in anyone's life.

Ideally, this course should be taught one-on-one as this has the greatest impact on the new disciple. It can also be taught in very small groups if, for some reason, this is not practical. Although it can be taught straight through, we generally envision that the lessons be taught over a 12-week period. We have an Instructor's Guide on CD-ROM available (which includes PowerPoints for each chapter) to help those who teach the course to do so as effectively as possible. This course is designed to be a gateway course, and is available from Church of God Men's Discipleship at (www.lifebuilderscog.com).

It is our hope and prayer that this course will be a blessing to Christian men and will help "...to prepare God's people for works of service, so that the body of Christ may be built up until we all reach unity in the faith and in the knowledge of the Son of God and become mature, attaining to the whole measure of the fullness of Christ" (Ephesians 4:12,13).

Patrick Morley
Leonard Albert
Don Warrington

Table of Contents

Lesson 1: What It Means to Be a Christian

(Subject: Salvation)

> *Man's search for meaning is the primary motivation in his life* (Viktor Frankl, *Man's Search for Meaning*).
>
> *There is a God-shaped vacuum in the heart of every man, which only God can fill through His Son, Jesus Christ* (Blaise Pascal, *Pensées*).
>
> *Thou hast made us for thyself, and the heart of man is restless until it finds itself in thee* (Augustine, *Confessions*).

Memory Verse for This Lesson

> *I am the Way, the Truth, and the Life. No one comes to the Father except through me* (John 14:6).

Introduction

Many men find they have a lingering feeling that something isn't quite right about their lives. They have been living by their own ideas, and their lives are not turning out the way they planned. They often feel overwhelmed by life. When is the last time you thought to yourself, *Is this all there is? There* must *be more to life ... there's gotta be.*

The history of human thought has focused around one central question: What is the meaning of things, and the purpose of life? Down through the ages men have continually tried to draw a circle big enough to explain the meaning and purpose of life.

To find the meaning of life is the task of sorting things out, of finding a meaningful philosophy of life, of building a system that fits the bits and pieces of life into a unified, sensible whole. Christians are the only group on earth who have a complete circle, a system of truth to explain life.

Man's greatest need is the need to be significant—to have purpose.

Men are looking for a cause, a mountain to climb, a challenge, a mission in life, something worthy of making a sacrifice to accomplish, a world to change and conquer. Only Christians find a purpose in life big enough to satisfy.

The Person and Work of Jesus Christ

What Is a Christian?

Words often become spoiled of their originally intended meaning. C.S. Lewis in his 1943 book, *Mere Christianity,* pointed out that the word *gentleman* originally meant something exact—to have a coat of arms and own property. To be called a gentleman, then, was not a compliment, but a statement of fact. Over time, however, the term evolved into a way of complimenting a man, instead of giving information about him. As a result, as Lewis pointed out, *gentleman* is now useless for its original meaning—it has been spoiled for that purpose.

The term *Christian* has also evolved to mean different things to different people. Ask ten different people what it means to be a Christian and you are likely to receive 12 different answers. In fact, *Webster's Encyclopedic Unabridged Dictionary* actually does carry 12 different definitions for the word *Christian.* According to the Bible, however, there is only one definition of a Christian: a person who has responded to the gospel of Jesus Christ and has been reconciled to God through repentance and faith in Jesus Christ as Savior and Lord. Let us examine the different parts of this definition.

Identity: Who Is Jesus?

The truth about Jesus Christ is not based upon feelings or impressions about Him, or based on the hearsay of others. Rather, the Bible is the historical and factual record of His life.

If you were considering an investment, you would listen to opinions and observe who else was making the investment. However, the facts (truth) about the investment would be contained in the prospectus, which is the document that describes in detail the investment being offered. If you wanted to know the truth, you would read the prospectus.

The Bible is the prospectus on Jesus Christ. If you want to consider the life of Jesus Christ, the Bible is where the facts are. *Read the following passages from the Bible that discuss who Jesus Christ is, and write down what you observe:*

Colossians 1:15-20

____

____

____

____

Hebrews 1:1-4

____

____

____

____

John 1:1-14

____

____

____

What are the most prominent facts about Jesus in these verses? Put an asterisk by those that are new to you.

Answer the following questions by writing the correct answers in your own words from the indicated Bible verses.

1) Who did Jesus say He was? Initially, people were confused about who Jesus was. However, as time passed His identity became clear to those who sought to know Him.

a) John 4:25, 26

b) John 10:30

c) John 14:6

d) John 14:9

2) What does the term "Messiah" mean?

J.B. Phillips in *Your God Is Too Small* said, "It is impossible to avoid the conclusion that He believed Himself to be God." Do you agree or disagree? Why or why not?

3) Who did people think Jesus was?

a) John 6:14, 15

b) Matthew 16:13, 14

c) Matthew 16:15, 16

A comment from C.S. Lewis will help put these facts in perspective:

A man who was merely a man and said the sort of things Jesus said would not be a great moral teacher. He would either be a lunatic-on a level with the man who says he is a poached egg—or else he would be the Devil of Hell. You must make your choice. Either this man was, and is, the Son of God; or else a madman or something worse. You can shut Him up for a fool, you can spit at Him and kill Him as a demon; or you can fall at His feet and call Him Lord and God. But let us not come with any patronizing nonsense about His being a great human teacher. He has not left that open to us. He did not intend to.[1]

4) What do you think? Who do you say Jesus is?

His Purpose: Why Did He Come?

From the following verses, piece together the story of why Jesus came:

- Luke 19:10

____

- John 6:40

____

- John 10:10

____

- John 15:10b

____

- Romans 5:7, 8

____

- 1 John 2:2

____

Jesus became a man for one overarching purpose. He came to seek and to save those who were lost. Jesus is the Messiah, the Savior, who came to give eternal life to those who believe. He came to perform two principal tasks.

- First, to live a sinless life of perfect obedience to the Father
- Second, to voluntarily substitute Himself in our place to

die for our sins, the just for the unjust, the obedient for the disobedient, the sinless for the sinful. Jesus came to die on an old, rugged cross.

According to the record of the Bible, Jesus was born of a virgin, was crucified for our sins, was buried, and was raised from the dead. These historical facts are what we call the *gospel*, or good news.

Read 1 Corinthians 15:3-8.

1) What level of importance did Paul attribute to these historical facts?

____

____

____

____

2) Who were the witnesses to Christ's resurrection?

____

____

____

____

How to Have a Relationship With God

Once you realize that you will not have eternal life unless you accept Jesus Christ as your Lord and Savior, there are four essential things that you must consider. Write down the verses and take a careful look at the following:

1. God's Position

John 3:16

____

- God loves man and wants to have fellowship with him. The best-known, most-quoted scripture in the Bible—which you wrote down above—assures us that He loved us so much that He sent His only Son to die for our sins. If we accept that, He will restore that which we lost through Adam.
- God's position is also one of perfection and His character and holiness will not allow Him to lower His standards. This leaves us with a dilemma that is impossible to solve—unholy people standing before a holy God.

2. Man's Condition

Romans 3:23

Romans 6:23

- All people have sinned and fallen short of God's standard. Some people may think they come pretty close, but if you asked them to reveal their every thought in the last 24-hour period, they would fall back in line with everyone else.
- Some people do live better lives than others. If we were all swimmers who wanted to swim to Hawaii, some wouldn't get far at all while others might go for many miles. The truth is, none would make it to Hawaii. All would fall way short of the goal. This is similar to trying to provide for our own salvation.
- It is pride working at its peak that allows us to think we can get there by our own plan or action.
- God in His justice, requires the penalty of eternal separation from Him.
- God wants us to be with Him, but He won't lower the standard.

We want to be with Him but we don't meet the standard. This seems to be a bleak and impossible situation.

3. God's Provision

John 1:29

___

2 Corinthians 5:21

___

- Hang on, help is on the way! Jesus Christ, being God, paid the penalty for our sins by dying on the cross as our substitute. He made it possible for us to have a personal relationship with Him by offering Himself, the perfect sacrifice, in exchange for our sins.
- An illustration: "A young man by the name of Goldstein was charged with drunken driving, and the judge who was to hear his case was his father. His father had a reputation as the 'hanging judge,' always giving out the full penalty for an offense. A question was raised: 'Will the "hanging judge" hang his own son?' The day of the trial, the judge asked his son how he pled. 'Guilty, your honor.' The judge proceeded to give him the maximum fine of $5,000. He then rose from behind the bench, removed his judiciary robe and came down and stood next to his son. He said, 'I am a just judge and require the full demands of the law for your offense, but I'm also your father and I am going to pay the penalty for you.' With that he reached into his pocket and pulled out a $5,000 check." (*State of California v. Goldstein*) In this substitutionary setting, justice was served and love was manifested. That is what Jesus did for us!
- That is why John the Baptist called Jesus the "Lamb of God" referring to the sacrificial Lamb who would free all of us forever.

4. Man's Decision

John 1:12

Ephesians 2:8, 9

- On the top of a hill in a Midwestern state stands a courthouse so situated that raindrops fall from its roof into two different bodies of water. On one side of the roof they travel by way of the Great Lakes into the Atlantic, while drops landing on the opposite side find their way through the Ohio and Mississippi rivers to the Gulf of Mexico. Just a breath of wind one way or the other may determine whether a single raindrop will end up in the Gulf or in the Atlantic. One single decision is enough to determine man's destiny, either heaven or hell.
- We have established who God is and what He is able to provide. We have shown what man needs and what he cannot provide. We have looked into the provision God has made available for us, and now we face that decision. You must now answer the question, "What are you going to do with the information you have?"
- All you must do is place your trust in Christ and accept His death as necessary and sufficient payment for sin. This satisfies God's requirement of perfection and establishes His desired eternal relationship with man.
- A life-changing decision is needed to change a life.

Receiving Salvation

Receiving salvation is more than a casual nod to a stated proposition. It is a complete surrender—a surrender of intellect, will and life—to God himself. As A.W. Tozer said:

> *The trouble is that the whole "accept Christ" attitude is likely to be wrong. It shows Christ applying to us*

> *rather than us to Him. It makes Him stand hat in hand awaiting our verdict instead of our kneeling with troubled hearts awaiting His verdict on us. It may even permit us to accept Christ by an impulse of mind or emotions, painlessly, at no loss to our ego and no inconvenience to our usual way of life.*

It is one thing to believe intellectually that the stock market will go up. It is a whole different matter to purchase stock and put your faith and resources—yourself, in reality—in that belief. Once you know that Jesus Christ is who He said He is, and that He has done what He says He has done, you can be reconciled with God personally through Christ by doing two things:

First, you must acknowledge and confess your sins, purposing in your mind to repent, which means, "to think differently, to turn around." It is a change of direction toward God. "If we claim to be without sin, we deceive ourselves and the truth is not in us. If we confess our sins, He is faithful and just and will forgive us our sins and purify us from all unrighteousness" (1 John 1:8, 9).

Second, you must submit to Jesus Christ by faith as both Savior and Lord. You must receive Him: "Yet to all who received Him, to those who believed in His name, He gave the right to become children of God" (John 1:12). The Spirit of Christ literally enters your life when you place your faith in Him. He is the way to God. As we noted at the beginning, Jesus said, "I am the way—and the truth and the life. No one comes to the Father except through me" (John 14:6).

How does one receive Him? By faith. Faith is trusting God. Faith is believing that Jesus is who He says He is—the Savior. That He did what He says He did—paid the penalty for our sins. And, that He will do for us what He says He will do—forgive our sins and give us eternal life.

What if, after completing this study, you realize you have never trusted Christ by faith? Men are generally wired to be proactive. They think that they can accomplish their goals in life by doing. Men frequently make a complete wreck of their lives by attempting to achieve what they do not have the resources to do. Perhaps you have been wrongly working your way toward heaven. Are you sensing a desire to repent and trust Jesus Christ now? If you are, that is the Holy Spirit quickening you to give you the desire. "Flesh gives birth to flesh, but the Spirit gives to spirit" (John 3:6).

If you have never actually placed your faith in Christ you may be thinking, *Okay, I'm interested. But how? How do I actually express this faith?* You can express faith and receive it by willfully surrendering your life to Him. Jesus said, "Here I am! I stand at the door and knock. If anyone hears my voice and opens the door, I will come in and eat with him, and he with Me" (Revelation 3:20).

How does one make such a willful surrender? You can make a willful surrender of your life to Jesus Christ by faith through prayer. Prayer is simply expressing your thoughts to God. Here is a suggested prayer to repent and place your trust in Jesus Christ:

> *Lord Jesus, I need You. Thank You for dying on the cross for my sins, which I acknowledge and confess. I open the door of my life and invite You to come in. By faith, I believe and submit to You as my Savior and Lord. Thank You for forgiving my sins and for giving me eternal life. Take control of my life and make me into the kind of person You want me to be. Amen.*

Does this prayer express the desire of your heart, mind and will? If it does and you have never trusted Christ, let me encourage you to kneel, pray to God, and settle the issue of your eternal destiny this very moment.

Assurance: How Can Anyone Be Sure?

Once you become a Christian, can you lose it? The sincere Christian may still find himself doubting whether or not he is really saved. This is not at all unusual or abnormal. However, all Christians can have an assurance of their salvation. The longer one walks with Christ the greater this sense of eternal security will become, though you can have it from the very beginning.

If you have received Christ, you can gain an assurance three ways:

1) *By the Word.* The Word of God is the final rule of authority in the life of a Christian. *What does the Bible say about the security of your salvation?*

   - John 6:47

     ____

   - John 10:27-29

     ____

   - Philippians 1:6

     ____

   - 1 John 5:11, 12

     ____

2) *By faith.* We are saved by grace through faith. "We live by faith, not by sight" (2 Corinthians 5:7). "Without faith it is impossible to please God" (Hebrews 11:6). The opposite is true—we do not live by feelings. We gain an assurance through living by faith in God's Word and not trusting in changing emotions.

3) *By the internal testimony of the Holy Spirit.* The authority of Scripture is the basis of our assurance. The Scriptures say, "The Spirit himself testifies with our spirit that we are God's children" (Romans 8:16). If you have received Christ, shut your eyes and say to yourself: *I belong to Jesus. I am a child of God.*

Do you sense harmony with that thought? That is the Spirit testifying with your spirit that you are a child of God. He loves you with an everlasting love. You belong to Him. He approves of you. He made you. The sense of assurance swelling within you is the Spirit himself testifying with your own spirit that you are born again. You can have assurance of your relationship with God.

A Final Reflection: Christian Paradox

> *A Christian is an odd bird anyway. He feels supreme love for someone he has never seen, talks familiarly every day to someone he cannot see, expects to go to heaven on the virtue of another, empties himself in order to be made full, admits he is wrong so he can be declared right, goes down in order to get up, is strongest when he is weakest, richest when he is poorest, dies so that he can live, forsakes in order to have, gives away in order to keep, seeks the invisible, hears the inaudible, and knows things that are beyond knowledge (*A. W. Tozer).

[1] C.S. Lewis, *Mere Christianity*, p. 56.

Lesson 2: Knowing and Conforming to God's Character

(Subjects: Self-Examination, Character of God)

> *Nearly all wisdom we possess, that is to say, true and sound wisdom, consists of two parts: the knowledge of God and of ourselves (*John Calvin).
>
> *Nothing is easier than self-deceit, for what each man wishes that he also believes to be true (*Demosthenes).

Memory Verse for This Lesson

> *Since the creation of the world God's invisible qualities his eternal power and divine nature—have been clearly seen, being understood from what has been made . . .* (Romans 1:20).

Most men who come to faith in Jesus Christ bring a plan for their lives or some ambitions along with them. These vested interests can distort how we see God. We tend to have preconceived ideas about who God is, what we want Him to be like, and what we want Him to do for us.

However, God is who He is, and doesn't change. Our task, then, is not to press God into the mold of our expectations but to come humbly before Him, searching for the truth about God, as He exists.

In doing business with someone new, one of the first tasks is to get to know the person—to get a "feel" for him. What is his character? What makes him tick? What is his personality? What does he like, and dislike? How can he be pleased? What is he like in different situations? Doing business with God is no different. What is God like? And, how do we get to know Him? There are two steps:

Step 1: Self-examination

Get to know yourself. Knowledge of self is the gate to knowing God.

> *After all is considered, the number one shortcoming of man at the close of the twentieth century (as it has been at the close of every century) is that we lead unexamined lives. Most men have not carefully chiseled their life view by a personal search for truth and obedience to God* (Patrick M. Morley, *The Man In The Mirror*).

> *The life which is unexamined is not worth living* (Plato).

Through the self-deceit that comes from leading an unexamined life, many men find themselves following the God they want, and not the God who is.

> *There is a God we want, and there is a God who is—and they are not the same God. The turning point of our lives is when we stop seeking the God we want and start seeking the God who is* (Patrick M. Morley).

By selectively reading only those Bible verses that agree with our preconceived notions and expectations and by ignoring those that disagree, we can create a sort of "fifth gospel"—Matthew, Mark, Luke, John, and ______________________________ (insert your name).

To open yourself up to the knowledge of self is the first crucial step to learning about the character of God. Unless we look at our own lives in the mirror of self-examination, then blind spots, weak spots, and the pride that comes when we have more answers than questions will cripple us. Humility leads to knowledge of God.

Take the self-examination located at *Figure* 1. How are you doing? Let your answers guide you as you seek to discover more about the God who is.

Figure 1 Self Examination

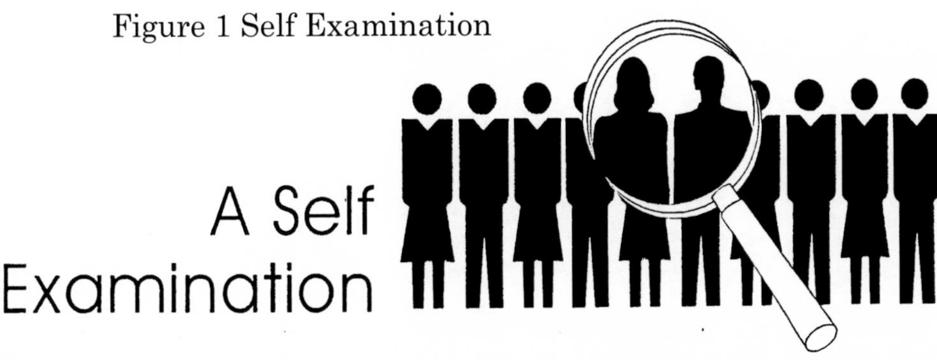

Reflect on the following continuums and place an **"X"** where you think you have been and a **"check mark"** where you would like to end up in the near future. Put an "*" next to the area needing the most attention.

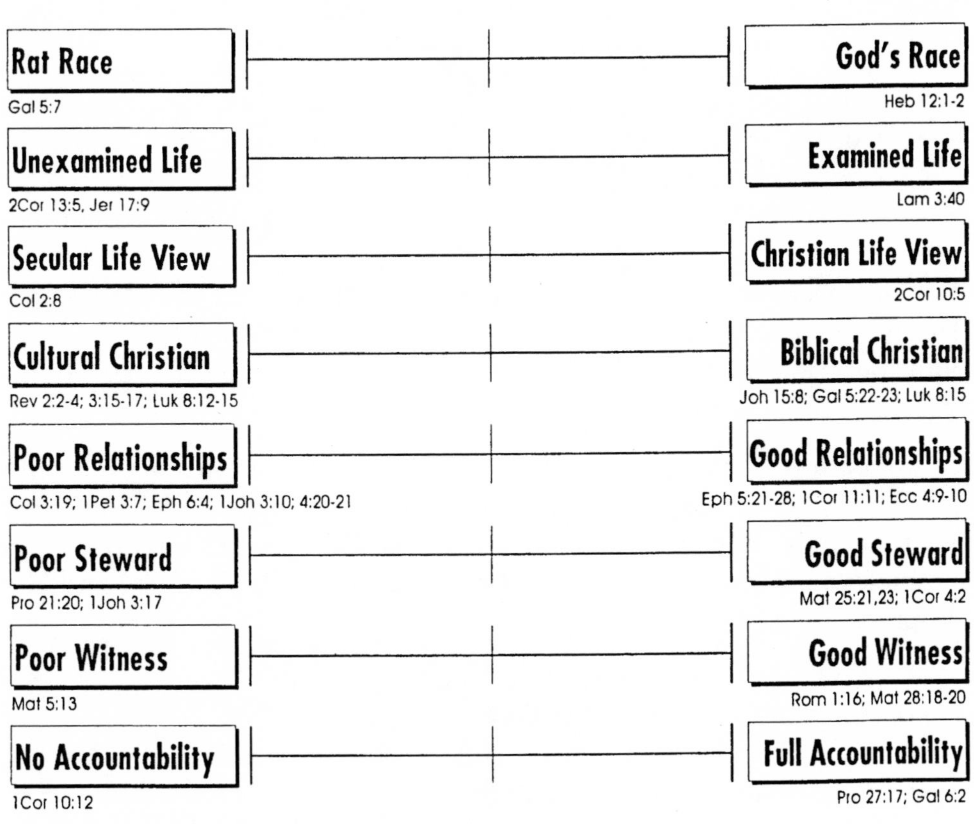

Step 2: Study the Attributes of God

Love the Lord your God with all of your ____________ *and with all of your* ________________ *and with all of your* ______________________ *and with all of your* ________________________ (Mark 12:30, fill in the blanks).

In other words, love God with the totality of your being. How can such a consuming love be possible? When you were first attracted to your wife or girlfriend you knew enough to be interested, but not enough to commit your life to her. Discuss the following:

- What happened to change your mind?
- Could knowing enough to get married be equated to knowing enough to accept Christ as Savior and Lord?
- Do knowledge of and love for each other stop growing at the moment of union?

To know God is to love Him, and to love Him is to want to know Him more intimately. If we desire to know the God who is, we must examine His character. Who is God? What is He like? How is He different from what we first imagined?

No undertaking will produce greater fruit in the life of a Christian than the study of the character and attributes of God: His holiness, His sovereignty, His unchanging nature, His power, His love, His goodness, His grace, His mercy, His faithfulness, His justice, and His happiness. He is:

- Immutable: He does not change
- Immortal: He is deathless
- Invisible: He cannot be seen
- Omnipotent: He has all power
- Omniscient: He knows everything
- Omnipresent: He is everywhere.

Let's explore several of His attributes and character. Begin by writing the indicated verse in your own words. Answer the questions on the blanks provided.

1. God Is Sovereign, 1 Chronicles 29:11, 12

God is sovereign because He is the supreme authority over all creation. He is not subject to any other power superior to Himself.

Every day millions of Christians throughout the world repeat the Lord's Prayer, "Your kingdom come, Your will be done on earth as it is in heaven" (Matthew 6:10). Some repeat it daily, others weekly, some only occasionally. How many might say it on a given Sunday? One hundred million? Five hundred million?

With so many of us praying, either God's will is, in fact, being done or God must not hear, or worse, not have the power to act.

The Bible is certain about God's sovereignty in the face of our uncertainty. What does Matthew 10:29 say about the sovereignty of God?

According to Ephesians 1:11, what percentage of things that happen are in conformity to the will of God?

The Bible claims without the slightest trace of hedging that God is completely, totally in control and that His will *is* being done in *everything.* No detail, no matter how minute, escapes the purpose of His sovereign will—not even the falling of a single sparrow.

2. God Is Creator, Revelation 4:11

Not only is God's rule sovereign, everything He rules is something He made.

> *The God who made the world and everything in it is the Lord of heaven and earth and does not live in temples built by hands. And he is not served by human hands, as if he needed anything, because he himself gives all men life and breath and everything else. From one man he made every nation of men, that they should inhabit the whole earth; and he determined the times set for them and the exact places where they should live. God did this so that men would seek him and perhaps reach out for him and find him, though he is not far from each one of us. "For in him we live and move and have our being"* (Acts 17:24-28).

He made the world and everything in it. He himself gives life, breath and everything else to all men whether believer or nonbeliever. His common grace extends to all men. Without His quickening, no man could draw a single breath. Without His air there would be nothing to breathe.

He determines the times which mark our birth and our death. Why were you born in this century and not the last? Or the next? He determines ... the exact places where we will live—the country, the culture, the community.

3. God Is Personal, Isaiah 57:15

Many believe in God, but think that He is distant, aloof, and impersonal. This is deism—to believe that God exists, but that He wound up the world, and now we are on our own. Deism is the belief of a Mason, not a Christian.

The Bible gives a markedly different report. God personally and individually created us. He is the first cause of everything and everyone:

> *For you created my inmost being; you knit me*

> *together in my mother's womb. I praise you because I am fearfully and wonderfully made; your works are wonderful, I know that full well. My frame was not hidden from you when I was made in the secret place. When I was woven together in the depths of the earth, your eyes saw my unformed body. All the days ordained for me were written in your book before one of them came to be* (Psalm 139:13-16).

God is not an impersonal being, but most personal. Not distant, He is intimately involved with every detail.

4. God Is Love, 1 John 4:16

God is 100 percent love. There is no time at which God is not love by His very being. Twenty-six times, Psalm 136 repeats the refrain: "His love endures forever." Everything God does is motivated by His character, which always includes love (John 3:16). He has promised no one can snatch us away from Him once we have believed (John 10:28). He is the good shepherd who lays down His life for His sheep (John 10:11). He died for our sins while we were still sinners (Romans 5:7, 8).

That God always loves does not mean that He is maudlin or permissive. The great love He has for the world is part of His nature. It is the perpetual disposition of His heart. He is slow to anger because He abounds in love.

Read the following passages slowly—they are wonderful reminders of His exquisite love:

- John 10:11,14,27, 28
- Romans 5:3-8
- Romans 8:35-39
- Ephesians 3:17-19

5. God Is Holy, Luke 1:49

God is 100 percent holy. God is 100 percent holy and 100 percent love 100 percent of the time. There is no time at which God is not holy. He is always simultaneously holy and loving.

Not only is God holy, He is "holy, holy, holy" (Isaiah 6:3). The Orthodox churches reflect a similar sentiment in their "Thrice-Holy Hymn": "Holy God, Holy Mighty, Holy Immortal, have mercy on us." In both cases not only is His holiness emphasized, but His nature as one God in three Persons is also illustrated. Words cannot adequately capture the intensity of His holiness, but several Bible stories give us a glimpse of the beauty and awesomeness of His holiness.

One such experience was the vision Ezekiel had of Christ. The purpose of a wedding processional is to elevate the moment, to create anticipation, to turn up the volume. Like a wedding processional, the living creatures described in the first chapter of Ezekiel pique anticipation for what is to come. After detailing the living creatures Ezekiel wrote:

> *Above the expanse over their heads was what looked like a throne of sapphire, and high above on the throne was a figure like that of a man. I saw that from what appeared to be his waist up he looked like glowing metal, as if full of fire, and that from there down he looked like fire; and brilliant light surrounded him....This was the appearance of the likeness of the glory of the LORD* (Ezekiel 1:26-28).

When Ezekiel saw the glory of the Lord did he run to greet Him? No, rather, "When I saw it, I fell facedown." Ezekiel is not the only man to have an encounter with the holiness of God and fall facedown, hide his face, or cry out in holy terror.

Others include Moses, Isaiah, Gideon, Joshua, Elijah, Job, Daniel, Peter, James, John, and Paul. Read about them in the following passages:

- *Moses*, Exodus 3:6
- *Joshua*, Joshua 5:14
- *Gideon*, Judges 6:22, 23
- *Elijah*, 1 Kings 19:12, 13
- *Job*, Job 42:5, 6
- *Isaiah*, Isaiah 6:5
- *Daniel*, Daniel 1:7-10
- *Peter*, Matthew 17:6
- *James*, Matthew 17:6
- *Paul*, Acts 9:4
- *John*, Revelation 1:17

What so repeatedly terrified these men when they found themselves in the presence of God? It was the awesome, dreadful presence of the holiness of God.

> *And the LORD said, "I will cause all my goodness to pass in front of you, and I will proclaim my name, the LORD, in your presence. I will have mercy on whom I will have mercy, and I will have compassion on whom I will have compassion. But," he said, "you cannot see my face, for no one may see me and live"* (Exodus 33:19, 20).

We are incapable of standing in God's presence on our own.

6. God Is Compassionate, Psalm 103:8

Considering that God drew you to Himself while "you were dead in your transgressions and sins" (Ephesians 2:1), the compassion of God becomes clear. How should this grace and kindness affect our attitude toward God?

---

7. God Is Forgiving, 1 John 1:9

God initiated the forgiveness of our sins through the atoning death of Jesus. "Very rarely will anyone die for a righteous man, though for a good man someone might possibly dare die. But God demonstrates his own love for us in this: While we were still sinners, Christ died for us" (Romans 5:7, 8). Is there anything you need to confess to God and ask His forgiveness for?

---

8. God Is Eternal, 1 Timothy 1:17

God is eternal because there has never been a time when God did not exist. He is without beginning or end.

9. God Is Immutable, Hebrews 13:8

God is immutable because He never changes. James 1:17 says that He "does not change like shifting shadows." What consolation can this give you?

---

10. God Is Omnipotent, Jeremiah 32:17

God has unlimited and absolute power and authority.

11. God Is Omnipresent, Jeremiah 23:23, 24

Because God is spirit, He can simultaneously be present everywhere at once.

12. God Is Omniscient, Psalm 139:2-4

God knows all things because of His unlimited knowledge and wisdom. As the Egyptian church father, Origen, put it, "For the divine nature knows the secret thoughts which revolve in our minds."[1] Why do we sometimes think we can do things in secret? Can we?

---

13. God Is Righteous, Psalm 145:17

God's nature is to only do what is good and right and never to do wrong.

14. God Is Just, 2 Thessalonians 1:6, 7

By His very nature, God cannot be unfair. He has committed Himself to perfect justice, mitigated to us by the mercies of His grace through the shed blood of Christ Jesus. Are you as grateful for God's love and forgiveness as you ought to be? Why, or why not?

---

15. God Is Truthful, John 18:37

By God's nature it is impossible for Him to lie (see Titus 1:2). His word is truth (see John 17:17).

16. God Is Happy, 1 Timothy 1:11

The word *blessed* in Greek is the word for *happy*. God is supremely happy! "He who is perfect is happy, for He knows His perfection…O God, I rejoice in your eternal happiness!"[2] Moreover, He wants us to be happy as well: "Taste and see that the LORD is good; blessed [happy] is the man who takes refuge in him (Psalm 34:8).

Conclusion

Obviously, we cannot fully explore each attribute of God and

His character in this short space. A suggestion: Make a life-long file on each attribute of God, study Him, listen to tapes, attend special conferences, make sermon notes, copy meaningful quotes, scribble notes on napkins and put them all on file. Make a life-long commitment to constantly learn and personally experience God's character and beauty. *Experience with God is the only way to move our understanding of Him from abstract to personal.*

When we do begin to plumb the depth and richness of each attribute or characteristic of God, that attribute will have a profound impact upon our beliefs, our doctrine, our faith, our practices, our motivations, and our daily lives—increasingly so as we move along the spectrum from the cold blues of abstract to the warm golden tones of personal experience.

Over the long haul, God will draw each of us to know Him as He is. As a friend says, "We pursue God out of priority or pain." Too many men like to put the really important things off until later. But later assumes that we'll be able to do in the future what we could do now. Don't wait until things are really bad. Make knowing God a priority.

A Final Reflection

- He slept with the windows open.
- He stuck to a diet with plenty of fresh vegetables.
- He relinquished his tonsils and traded in several worn out glands.
- He golfed—but never more than 18 holes at a time.
- He got at least eight hours' sleep every night.
- He never smoked, drank or lost his temper.
- He did his "daily dozen" daily. He was all set to live to be a hundred.

The funeral will be held Wednesday. He's survived by eight specialists, three health institutions, two gymnasiums and numerous manufacturers of health foods. He forgot God.

[1] Origen, *On First Principles*, 4, 37
[2] Jaques Benigne Bossuet, *Elevations on the Mysteries*, 1,3.

Lesson 3: Spending Quality Time With God

(Subjects: Bible, Prayer, Change, Quality Time)

> *In twenty-five years, the Bible will be a forgotten book (*Robert Ingersoll, deceased 1899).
>
> *Most people are bothered by those passages in Scripture which they cannot understand. The Scripture which troubles me most is the Scripture I do understand (*Mark Twain, deceased 1910).
>
> *Another century and there will not be a Bible on earth (*Voltaire, deceased 1778).
>
> *I did not take up the pen to teach you the thoughts of men (*Jaques-Bénigne Bossuet, *Elevations on the Mysteries).*
>
> *The grass withers and the flowers fall, but the word of the Lord stands forever* (Isaiah 40:8).

Memory Verse for This Lesson

> *All Scripture is God-breathed and is useful for teaching, rebuking, correcting and training in righteousness* (2 Timothy 3:16).

Why Do We Need Quality Time With God?

One of the plagues of modern life is that we do not spend quality time with anyone—not even our wives or children. Quality time is an essential ingredient in any relationship. If we want our relationship with God to grow and bring us happiness in this life and the next, we must spend quality time with God.

Christianity is all about change, and not just change but radical change. To be born again means that the old man dies and a new man in Christ comes to life. But that change does not stop with our initial salvation experience. When the apostle Paul became a Christian he made changes in four key areas: *tasks, relationships, thinking,* and *plans.* Even so, these changes took many years to come to full fruition.

When a man gives his life to Christ, the Lord Jesus will transform that man's life in direct proportion to the degree which that man yields and surrenders his life to the sanctifying grace of the Father. Much of this transformation comes by the renewing of the mind. "Do not conform any longer to the pattern of this world, but be transformed by the renewing of your mind. Then you will be able to test and approve what God's will is—his good, pleasing and perfect will" (Romans 12:2). How do we renew the mind? Much of this transforming work takes place during the quality time we spend with God.

> *I have never met a man whose life has changed in any significant way apart from the regular study of God's Word. A man who would change his world must by his Bible first be changed* (Patrick M. Morley).

Does the Bible tell us to spend quality time with God? What do the following verses suggest?

1. Bible Reading, Psalm 1:1-3:

   ____

2. Bible Study, 2 Timothy 3:16, 17:

   ____

3. Prayer, Philippians 4:6, 7:

   ____

The Bible clearly demonstrates the need for quality time with our Creator and Savior. In this lesson we will describe two ways we do this:

1. Bible reading and study
2. Prayer.

Why Read and Study the Bible?

The Bible consists of 66 separate books written on three continents, in three languages, over a 1500-year time span by 37 human authors inspired by the Holy Spirit. These included kings and peasants, philosophers and fishermen, poets and statesmen, shepherds and soldiers. Even with such remarkable diversity, the Scriptures by far possess the greatest unity and continuity among the great works of literature.

Manuscript evidence harpoons criticism on that front. Whereas only five complete manuscripts of Aristotle and 12 of Plato exist, 13,000 New Testament manuscripts have survived the centuries. There is not room to mention in detail archaeological evidence such as the Dead Sea Scrolls and the uncovering of forgotten kingdoms whose only record is the Bible. Neither does space allow us to mention in detail 300 fulfilled prophesies made 400 to 1500 years before Christ's first coming, the track record of the Bible's benefits to men and societies, nor the testimony of its authors.

Now let us turn to the internal claims of the Bible. The Bible claims to be the authoritative, infallible Word of God. Complete the following sentences after looking up the indicated verses.

1. God is the source of all ____________________(2 Timothy 3:16).

From this verse list the four purposes for which Scripture is useful.

- a ________________ (See also Romans 15:4.)
- b ________________ (See also Hebrews 4:12.)
- c ________________ (See also 1 Corinthians 10:11.)
- d ________________ (See also Psalm 19:7.)

2. The Word of God is ________________ (Proverbs 30:5, 6).
3. The Word of God is ________________ (Matthew 24:35).
4. The Word of God is ________________ (Isaiah 55:11).

5. The Word of God is ________________ (John 17:17).

6. The Word of God reveals the way to ________________ (John 20:31).

7. The Bible gives believers assurance of their ________________ (1 John 5: 13).

So why do we read and study the Bible? Because it is the eternal, true, inerrant Word of God. It reveals the way to everlasting life through Jesus Christ. As the English reformer John Jewel put it, "Seeing then the key, whereby the way and entry to the kingdom of God is opened unto us, is the word of the Gospel and the expounding of the Law and the Scriptures, we say plainly, where the same word is not, there is not the key."[1]

Bible reading and study produces many earthly benefits as well. Read Psalm 1:1-3, and then answer these questions:

What kind of man is blessed?

____

In what does he delight?

____

How much does he meditate on the Word?

____

What will happen to him as a result?

____

Read Joshua 1:8. What happens to the man who (a) reads and studies the Bible daily and (b) obeys the Word of God?

____

The new Christian was asked to describe how he fought against the temptation to fall back into sin. He put it this way, "There is a real conflict raging within me between good and evil. It is like two dogs fighting." A friend asked how he knew which one was winning. His reply was, "The one I feed the most!"

George Mueller, the remarkably successful organizer of children's orphanages in Bristol, England, attributed much of his success to reading the Bible:

> *I believe that one of the chief reasons that I have been kept in happy useful service is that I have been a lover of Holy Scripture. It has been my habit to read the Bible through four times a year; in a prayerful spirit, to apply it to my heart, and practice what I find there. I have been for sixty-nine years a happy man; happy, happy, happy.*

Happy, happy, happy! Can you say that of your own life? Wouldn't that be a wonderful direction in which to aim the rest of your life? Few of us may feel led to read the Bible through four times a year, but how about a page a day? No matter what your current amount of reading is, almost all of us would benefit by devoting more time to daily Bible reading and study.

The people who make the greatest shipwreck of their faith are the people who don't think Biblically—even though they are Christians. To study the Bible is to learn the mind of God. To be willfully ignorant of the Bible is to invite disaster.

The Bible contains the big picture of God's will. The Bible also contains many specific principles of daily living. Should I sue a fellow Christian? Can I divorce my spouse for abandoning me? Can I marry a divorced person? What should be my attitude toward an unethical employer? These are not easy questions, but they do have answers—answers that are found in the Bible.

Historically, whenever the people of God have been gripped by the earthshaking doctrines of the Bible, they have set their worlds ablaze for the kingdom of God.

Why Pray?

Prayer is the currency of our personal relationship with Christ. It is the medium of exchange between needy people and a rich God. The man who is poor in relationships, destitute in hope, and hungry for significance can find them in prayer. "The prayer of a righteous man is powerful and effective" (James 5:16).

The foremost reason to pray is that Jesus prayed—He set the example. "But Jesus often withdrew to lonely places and prayed" (Luke 5:16). All the great heroes of the faith prayed. Abraham prayed. Moses prayed. Joseph prayed. Joshua prayed. Elijah prayed. Elisha prayed. Gideon prayed. Samuel prayed. David prayed. Peter prayed. John prayed. Paul prayed. Throughout history God has met with people who prayed to Him.

Another reason to pray is that we are invited to pray. What is the gist of Hebrews 4:16?

___

What does 1 Thessalonians 5:17 tell us about prayer?

___

According to Romans 8:26, what happens when we don't know what we ought to pray for?

___

What is our part in prayer and what is God's part?

Our Part

According to Matthew 21:22 our part is to:

___

According to John 16:24 we must ask:

___

> *...we can and should conclude all of our [prayers]...by Jesus Christ, Our Lord...for having nothing to ask from God except the results of His love, we truly ask "by Jesus Christ," if we believe with a firm and lively faith that He loves us by an outpouring of love which He has for His Son.*[2]

Matthew 7:7 says that if you ________________ it will be given to you.

That's it! Whatever need or desire we have, we bring it to Christ in faith, believing that *He is able.* When combined with the discipline of reading the Bible and actually listening to God, our desires will be synchronized with God's and we will receive what we ask because it is in His plan to start with.

God's Part

How will God respond to your prayers according to Matthew 7:9-11?

____

God's part is to answer all prayer in accordance with His will. When we are in tune with God's will, He listens to our prayers: "He listens to the godly man who does His will" (John 9:31).

Prayer is the most effective means possible to release the will of God. 1 John 5:14 tells us that if we ask anything according to His will:

____

Our God hears everything, of course. But He doesn't hear prayer outside His will in the sense that He doesn't *act* on it.

If we have asked for anything according to God's will, what will God then do according to 1 John 5:15?

____

Jesus' Teaching

List at least three important points from Jesus' teaching on prayer found in Matthew 6:5-15:

1. ____
2. ____
3. ____

God's Will

We often pray to know the will of God. We likely will pray two kinds of prayers when trying to discern the will of God: one when we know what we would like to happen, and another when we don't know.

The Prayer for a Specific Outcome

Some refer to the whole concept of praying for a specific outcome as prevailing prayer. The concept comes from scripture: "The prayer of a righteous man is powerful and effective" (James 5:16b). The idea of prevailing prayer is best stated by the 19th-century American preacher Charles G. Finney:

> *Prevailing, or effectual prayer, is prayer that attains the blessing that it seeks. It is that prayer that effectually moves God. The very idea of effectual prayer is that it effects its object.*[3]

When God firmly gives us the desire for a specific outcome then we should pray for it with all our hearts. We must understand, however, that "submission in prayer is acquiescence in the revealed will of God."[4] We can and should have confidence that God will do what is right, and in some cases that is all we can lift up to the throne room of God. But prevailing prayer is that which has a specific object that is known to be in the revealed will of God, and this kind of prayer is focused and frequently long.

What specific outcome are you praying for? Bring it in His name to the foot of the cross and lay it there.

The Prayer for Guidance

You stand at the fork in the road. Traffic is backed up. Everyone is waiting for you to make a decision. Which way do you go? Or do you do nothing? The prayer for guidance comes when a need surfaces but we do not yet sense God's definite leading.

Our prayers for God's will to be done are being answered in the private chambers of God, a place He invites us to come. "Let us then approach the throne of grace with confidence, so that we may receive mercy and find grace to help us in our time of need" (Hebrews 4:16).

If you are waiting for guidance and you don't sense it coming, wait for Him. Don't force the issue. Don't take matters into your own hands. God will supply the answer if you wait patiently for Him to act. As someone has said, "God is frequently early but never late."

The Prayer for Forgiveness

Nothing will sour our relationship with God faster than having unforgiven sin between Him and us. And none of us is exempt:

> *If we claim to be without sin, we deceive ourselves and the truth is not in us. If we confess our sins, he is faithful and just and will forgive us our sins and purify us from all unrighteousness. If we claim we have not sinned, we make him out to be a liar and his word has no place in our lives* (1 John 1:8-10).

In our prayer time, we need to keep our account short with God. While we are at it, we need to forgive others, not only because this is essential to our relationship with God but also to have our prayers answered:

> *Therefore I tell you, whatever you ask for in prayer, believe that you have received it, and it will be yours. And when you stand praying, if you hold anything against anyone, forgive him, so that your Father in heaven may forgive you your sins* (Mark 11:24, 25).

Why is it important that we seek forgiveness for our sins?

Structuring Our Quality Time With God

1. **When is the best time of the day to spend quality time with God?** This depends upon your own circumstances—it

is a personal decision. Factors include schedule, whether you are a day or night person, and other responsibilities. Most people have their quality time early in the morning or just before retiring for the evening. But you may prefer to set aside some time during lunch. The best schedule is the one you will follow.

2. **Where should you have your quality time with God?** This is a completely personal decision. You may find a desk, the kitchen table, or some other location that suits you best. If possible, be consistent. In the same way you learned it was valuable to have a regular place to do homework while in school, it is wise to have a regular place for your quality time with the Lord. One thing you might hear many people talk about is the "prayer closet." This is based on the following scripture: "But thou, when thou prayest, enter into thy closet, and when thou hast shut thy door, pray to thy Father which is in secret; and thy Father which seeth in secret shall reward thee openly" (Matthew 6:6, KJV). The idea behind a prayer closet is that wherever we spend quality time with God should be *a place without distractions*, so that we do not have to compete with other busyness for our attention.
3. **How often should you have quality time?** The Bible says that the person who *does* meditate on the Word daily "is like a tree planted by streams of water, which yields its fruit in season and whose leaf does not wither. Whatever he does prospers" (Psalm 1:3). The Bible also says, "Pray in the Spirit on all occasions with all kinds of prayers and requests" (Ephesians 6:18). The scriptures don't say we have to read the Bible and pray daily. Instead, they say we should *continually* meditate on the Word and pray about *everything*. The Biblical concept is *continual devotions*. Actually, the concept of a daily quality time is a cultural accommodation to busy, crowded schedules. Because most of us do have such hectic schedules, the idea of a few minutes devoted exclusively to Bible reading and prayer is valuable. Daily private devotions are not a *requirement,* but it is *wise*.

So how often should we have quality time? The best policy is to do so every day, or at least aim for a daily routine. Pick a time and place regular enough so you can reasonably make it about five of seven days a week.

4. **How long should quality time last?** If you have never had quality time with God before, consider establishing a maximum time limit for your devotional life, not a minimum. If you start with a minimum, you will spend your quality time watching the clock rather than listening to God. To begin with, start with a maximum of five minutes. If you pursue your quality time consistently, you will find yourself wanting to go on longer, increasing the maximum on a progressive basis. The idea is that your time will be driven by your desire to be with God. If you will set realistic expectations in the beginning, then your program has a better chance of success.
5. **What should you do during your quality time?** Bible reading, study, and prayer comprise the essentials of a quality time. Beginners may start by reading one chapter of the New Testament and praying a prayer (like the Lord's Prayer). If you read one chapter of the New Testament five days each week you will complete it in one year (260 chapters). As you progress you can include a program to read the Bible through over the course of a year. Guides are available through Christian bookstores, or you may purchase a *One Year Bible* organized into 365 daily readings. Many read the Bible through once every year.

   The acronym ACTS may be a helpful aid to prayer.
   - "A" is for adoration—praising God for His attributes.
   - "C" is for confession—asking forgiveness for the sins you have committed. Learn to keep short accounts with God.
   - "T" is for thanksgiving—expressing gratitude for His blessing and answers to prayers.
   - "S" is for supplication—asking for anything and everything that comes to mind for yourself and for others. Be persistent in prayer.

Lorne Sanny, former president of the Navigators, offers an incredibly useful suggestion for prayer. "Each day pray backwards through the day step-by-step. Do this expressing gratitude to God. Then pray forward through the day step-by-step. Make your requests known to Him." Why not give it a try?

6. **What else can you do during quality time?** You can be creative with how you spend your quality time. The essential parts are Bible reading and prayer. Beyond that, you can include keeping a journal, singing, meditating on scripture, reading scripture aloud, memorizing scripture (see Psalm 119:9-11), praying and reading aloud with your spouse, reference materials (e.g. commentaries), and reading prepared devotional materials.

Application

What kind of initial commitment to having a regular quality time is realistic for you?

What's your next step?

A Final Reflection: The Five-Finger Prayer

1) Your thumb is nearest to you. So begin your prayers by praying for those closest to you. They are the easiest to remember. To pray for our loved ones is, as C. S. Lewis once said, a "sweet duty."

2) The next finger is the pointing finger. Pray for those who teach, instruct and heal. This includes teachers, doctors, and ministers. They need support and wisdom in pointing others in the right direction. Keep them in your prayers.

3) The next finger is the tallest finger. It reminds us of our leaders. Pray for the president, leaders in business and industry, and

administrators. These people shape our nation and guide public opinion. They need God's guidance.

4) The fourth finger is our ring finger. Surprising to many is the fact that this is our weakest finger, as any piano teacher will testify. It should remind us to pray for those who are weak, in trouble or in pain. They need your prayers day and night. You cannot pray too much for them.

5) And lastly comes our little finger, the smallest finger of all—which is where we should place ourselves in relation to God and others. As the Bible says, "the least shall be the greatest among you." Your pinky should remind you to pray for yourself. By the time you have prayed for the other four groups, your own needs will be put into proper perspective and you will be able to pray for yourself more effectively.

---

[1] Jewel, John. *An Apology of the Church of England.* Translated by Lady Ann Bacon. Edited by J.E. Booty (Ithaca, New York: Cornell University Press, 1963). Originally published 1564.

[2] Jaques Bénigne Bossuet, *Meditations on the Gospel.*

[3] Charles G. Finney, *The Revivals of Religion* (Virginia Beach, Virginia: CBN University Press, 1978) p. 46.

[4] Ibid, p. 49.

Lesson 4: Living in the Spirit

(Subjects: The Holy Spirit, Sanctification, Baptism in the Holy Spirit)

> *Although every believer has the Holy Spirit, the Holy Spirit does not have every believer (*A. W Tozer).
>
> *The fruit of the Spirit is love, joy, peace, patience, kindness, goodness, faithfulness, gentleness and self-control (*Galatians 5:22, 23).

Memory Verse for This Lesson

> *Do not get drunk on wine, which is debauchery. Instead, be filled with the Spirit* (Ephesians 5:18).

The main reason why we spent the last lesson on our quality time with God is that our lives in Christ aren't just the initial experience of salvation followed by us being in a "holding tank" waiting for eternity. It is a process of growth and development. That process cannot take place without the presence of the Holy Spirit in the life of the believer. The ministry of the Holy Spirit is a core teaching of the Christian life. It's about getting control of the things that have control of you. If you miss this, you really miss the mark.

Who Is the Holy Spirit?

The Holy Spirit is God. The Holy Spirit is "He," not "It." He is the third person of the Trinity. In describing the Spirit in John 16:7-14, Jesus refers to the Spirit as "him" or "he" ten times.

To authenticate the *divinity* of the Holy Spirit in your own mind, write down the way each of the following verses identifies the Holy Spirit:

Romans 8:9: The Spirit is ________. He is also ________________.

2 Corinthians 3:17: The ________________is the Spirit.

John 4:24: __________________is Spirit.

In your own words, then, who is the Holy Spirit?

The Holy Spirit plays vital *roles* in the life of a believer. From the following verses identify the role of the Spirit. (You may want to use a one-word description or a phrase.)

1. John 14:16, 26; 16:7

   ---

2. John 16:8

   ---

3. John 16:13

   ---

4. Acts 1:8

   ---

5. Romans 8:26, 27

Of which roles have you not taken full benefit? What effect do you think your "nonuse" has had? What steps can you take to change things?

The Work of the Holy Spirit in Our Lives

Looked at from a timeline standpoint, the Christian life can be best seen as a process punctuated by important events. The most important of these is salvation—the moment when we ask Jesus Christ to come into our lives and rule as Lord and Savior. Once this takes place, the Holy Spirit comes into our lives and directs us in our spiritual growth. Without that direction we cannot develop the "mind of Christ."

Write down 1 Corinthians 2:14-16:

____

____

____

What advantages does the spiritual man have with the things of God?

____

____

Look up and copy James 1:8:

____

____

What happens when we are double-minded? What are the possible eternal consequences of such a state?

____

____

There are two central aspects of the work of the Holy Spirit in our lives that we will discuss:

1. Sanctification, or being made holy
2. Baptism in the Holy Spirit

Sanctification

The word *sanctification* simply means, "to make holy." We saw in Lesson 1 that the holiness of God—and our lack of it in our natural state—was an obstacle in our having a proper relationship with God. The 1662 *Book of Common Prayer* of the Church of England states that, to become a full member of the church, a believer must state the following: "Thirdly, in God the Holy Ghost, who sanctifieth me, and all the elect people of God." Sanctification is the spiritual kneading by the Holy Spirit of God's holiness into our lives.

There are misconceptions regarding sanctification, many of which are spread by well-meaning believers. The object of sanctification is God's holiness, and this requires that we walk in God's Spirit. You might think of it as walking a *Spiritual Balance Beam* (see Figure 1 below). When we are on the beam we are walking in the Spirit. When we choose to walk in the flesh we fall off the beam in one of two directions. Let's explore these possibilities.

Figure One
SPIRITUAL BALANCE BEAM

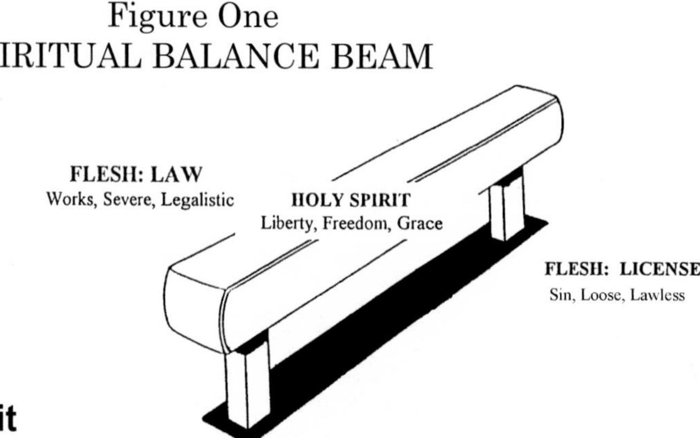

Walking in the Spirit

At its core, the normal Christian life is to walk in the fullness of the Holy Spirit. When we choose to live in the Spirit, our lives will (a) increasingly produce *the fruit of good works* (see Ephesians 2:10; John 15:8,16) and (b) increasingly exhibit *the fruit of the Spirit.* Look up Galatians 5:22, 23 and list the fruit of the Spirit:

1.____

2.____

3.____

4.____

5.____

6.____

7.____

8.____

9.____

When we choose, however, to walk in the flesh we fall off our *Spiritual Balance Beam* into one of two opposite errors—artificially trying to keep the *Law* or misusing our liberty through *license.* Let's look at these two errors further.

Walking in the Flesh

1. LAW

We are no longer under the Law. When we fall off our *Spiritual Balance Beam* on the side of being legalistic we *"under realize"* our new position in Christ and the Spirit. We are too severe and strict. We over emphasize works of the Law.

Many well-meaning Christians seem to think we are "saved by faith, but sanctified by works." They think being Christian means keeping a long list of rules and regulations—do's and don'ts. Nothing could be further from the truth. What is the central point of Colossians 2:20-23?

We are saved by faith and we are likewise sanctified by faith, not by obeying man-made laws, rules and regulations. What does Romans 7:6 tell us about our relationship to the Law?

The old way of the Law is to try to be good enough to deserve God's favor by doing the works of the Law. But no one can keep the Law: "For all have sinned and fall short of the glory of God" (Romans 3:23). So God gave us a new way to reconcile with Him through His Son, Christ Jesus. As a result, we have been released from the Law. We are to serve Him in the new way of the Spirit. We are not to again become bound up in trying to obey God by keeping the Law.

If we are released from the Law, does this mean the Ten Commandments are no longer important? Not at all. Jesus replaces the old written code with a new, higher standard. According to John 13:34, what is the new, higher standard of Christ?

Look up Romans 13:9, 10. What is the relationship between Christ's standard of love and the Law?

Matthew 22:40 in the *Living Bible* says about the commandments to love God with all your heart, mind and soul and to love your neighbor as yourself: "Keep only these and you will find that you are obeying all the others." Galatians 5:14 says, "The entire law is summed up in a single command: Love your neighbor as yourself.What do these verses tell us about the Law? (*NIV*).

____

Actually, when we live by the Spirit and obey Christ's law of love, we will find that we are keeping the Ten Commandments out of the overflow of our love, as a by-product of loving God and people.

Consider carefully the following two verses:

> *Are you so foolish? After beginning with the Spirit, are you now trying to attain your goal by human effort?* (Galatians 3:3).
>
> *It is for freedom that Christ has set us free. Stand firm, then, and do not let yourselves be burdened again by a yoke of slavery* (Galatians 5:1).

What should be our response to the temptation to please God by keeping the Law through works?

____

2. LICENSE

While we have been released from the Law, we are not to use our freedom to indulge the flesh (the flesh is also called "the sinful nature" and "the carnal nature"). When we fall off our *Spiritual Balance Beam* on the side of being licentious we *overrealize* our new position in Christ and the Spirit. We become loose and carnal. We take advantage of our freedom in Christ. What are the three points made in Galatians 5:13?

1. _______________________________________

2. _______________________________________

3. _______________________________________

What are the acts of the flesh (sinful nature) according to the following verses:

Galatians 5:19-21:

Colossians 3:8, 9

Mark 7:20-23

These lists of the acts of the flesh are *representative,* not *comprehensive.* Any sinful desire may be considered to come from the flesh.

The Baptism in the Holy Spirit

The baptism in the Holy Spirit is a defining experience for millions of Pentecostals, Charismatics, or those who adhere to the full gospel. Since modern Pentecost began at the turn of the 20th century, it has fueled revival and renewal throughout the earth.

But it is also a very misunderstood experience, both by those who believe in it and those who do not. Why do we need to be baptized in the Holy Spirit when we have been baptized with water? When we have received the Holy Spirit at salvation? At sanctification? And what benefits does God have for us in it?

To begin to answer these questions, the best place to start is where it all began—the original Day of Pentecost.

The Day of Pentecost

The original Day of Pentecost took place 50 days after the Passover of the Last Supper, where Jesus was betrayed on His way to the cross and resurrection, and ten days after Jesus had ascended into heaven. Those ten days saw the disciples and other followers of Jesus gathering and waiting. But waiting for what?

Acts 2:1-4

____

____

____

____

Questions for discussion:

1. How were these believers gathered? What does this signify?

   ____

2. Where did the violent wind and the tongues of fire come from? And where did they go?

   ____

3. Who enabled these people to "speak with other tongues"?

   ____

What the Baptism in the Holy Spirit Is Not

1. It is not primarily an emotional experience, although an emotional release with such an experience is entirely natural. It is not about *whipping up* feelings or emotions. When the initial release of tongues came, the first recorded emotions were of those who heard the tongues.
2. It is not entirely about speaking in tongues. Speaking in tongues is the initial evidence of the baptism in the Holy Spirit. The purpose of evidence is to prove the existence of something. The evidence in this case is to demonstrate to the believer and others that he has been baptized in the Holy Spirit.

What the Baptism in the Holy Spirit Is

1. The word *baptism* means "immersion." The normative form of baptism in the New Testament church—and for many years afterward, as it is today in many churches—is complete immersion of the believer in water. That's what the baptism in the Holy Spirit is all about—completely immersing the believer in the Holy Spirit.

2. The baptism in the Holy Spirit is from God. It is not about a special preacher coming to pray for you. It is not about making yourself do something. The baptism in the Holy Spirit is ultimately about empowerment—empowering you to do the work that God put you here to do, and principally to be a witness to others about what He has done for you (Acts 1:8).

Receiving the Baptism in the Holy Spirit

A fair number of urban legends have emerged about receiving the baptism in the Holy Spirit.

1. Some say that one must go to the altar to receive the baptism in the Holy Spirit. The altar at church is a good place to receive the baptism in the Holy Spirit, but is certainly not the only place.

2. Others believe that one must pray a certain way to receive the Baptism. But the 120 present at the first Pentecost were simply "all together in one place." They had been told to wait in Jerusalem to receive power from on high. They were not given a method to follow.

3. Still others have ideas as to how one should react to the Baptism. Beyond the initial evidence of tongues, the New Testament doesn't specify this either.

So How Can I Receive This Gift From God?

Below we have Charles R. Beach's "Power to Witness for Christ," which gives in detail the Biblical background for the baptism in the Holy Spirit and how you can receive it.

The baptism in the Holy Spirit is a life-changing experience, one you should not miss.

A Final Reflection

For the shooting of Ben Hur, Charlton Heston was training to drive a chariot. Heston was having trouble with the apparatus and said to his director, Cecil B. DeMille, "I can barely stay on this thing. I can't win the race." DeMille told Heston, "Your job is to stay on it. It's my job to make sure you win." The Holy Spirit orchestrates the victories for God's kingdom. Our job is to simply stay in the chariot of obedience.

Appendix: Power to Witness for Christ

Charles R. Beach and Terry Beavers

(All Scripture quotations in this appendix are from the King James Version.)

> *And with great power gave the apostles witness of the resurrection of the Lord Jesus* (Acts 4:33a).

The "uttermost part of the earth" has not yet been reached with the glorious gospel of Christ; "every creature" has not yet been told that Jesus alone saves from sin and hell. God needs powerful witnesses to carry out this task in these last days. Offer yourself as a witness and God will supply the power through His Holy Spirit. "Have ye received the Holy Ghost since ye believed?" (Acts 19:2).

Every Christian Is to Be a Witness

To witness for (to confess) Christ is the duty of every newly converted Christian and is a resultant phase of his conversion.

- *That if thou shalt confess with thy mouth the Lord Jesus, and shalt believe in thine heart that God hath raised him from the dead, thou shalt be saved* (Romans 10:9).

To witness for (to bear testimony of) Christ is a means of overcoming the devil.

- *And they overcame him [the devil] by the blood of the Lamb, and by the word of their testimony* (Revelation 12:11a).

To witness for Christ was the last commandment of the Lord.

- *And ye shall be witnesses unto me both in Jerusalem, and in all Judea, and in Samaria, and unto the uttermost part of the earth* (Acts 1:8b).

The Christian Needs Power to Be an Effective Witness for Christ

Christians receive power to become sons of God as a result of being born of the Holy Spirit (Holy Ghost)

- *But as many as received him, to them gave he power to become the sons of God, even to them that believe on his name: Which were born . . . of God* (John 1:12, 13). (Note also John 3:3-5.)

Christians receive power to witness for Christ as a result of the baptism (outpouring, gift, filling) in the Holy Ghost (Holy Spirit).

- *But ye shall receive power, after that the Holy Ghost is come upon you: and ye shall be witnesses unto me both in Jerusalem, and in all Judea, and in Samaria, and unto the uttermost part of the earth* (Acts 1:8).

The early followers of Christ and the apostles received this power to witness

- *And with great power gave the apostles witness of the resurrection of the Lord Jesus* (Acts 4:33a).

Paul, who was converted after the resurrection of Christ, received this power and a command to witness.

- *And Ananias went his way, and entered into the house; and putting his hands on him said, "Brother Saul, the Lord, even Jesus, that appeared unto thee in the way as thou camest, hath sent me, that thou mightest receive thy sight, and be filled with the Holy Ghost"* (Acts 9:17).
- *For thou shalt be his witness unto all men of what thou hast seen and heard* (Acts 22:15).

The Holy Ghost (Holy Spirit, Comforter) then is the real witness for Christ, working through the Christian.

- *But when the Comforter is come, whom I will send unto you from the Father, even the Spirit of truth, which proceedeth from the Father, he shall testify of me* (John 15:26).

The Holy Ghost aids the Christian to be an effective witness for Christ by bringing to his mind the words of Christ, the scriptures to be used.

- *But the Comforter, which is the Holy Ghost, whom the Father will send in my name, he shall teach you all things, and bring all things to your remembrance, whatsoever I have said unto you* (John 14:26).

The Baptism in the Holy Ghost, Which Brings Power to Witness, Was Foretold

The outpouring of the Holy Ghost was foretold by an Old Testament prophet.

- *And it shall come to pass afterward, that I will pour out my spirit upon all flesh; and your sons and your daughters shall prophesy, your old men shall dream dreams, your young men shall see visions: And also upon the servants and upon the handmaids in those days will I pour out my spirit* (Joel 2:28, 29). (Note fulfillment in Acts 2:16-21.)

The baptism in the Holy Ghost was foretold by John the Baptist

- *I indeed have baptized you with water: but he shall baptize you with the Holy Ghost* (Mark 1:8).

The gift of the Holy Ghost was foretold by Jesus

- *And I will pray the Father, and he shall give you another Comforter, that he may abide with you for ever; Even the Spirit of truth; whom the world cannot receive, because it seeth him not, neither knoweth him: but ye know him; for he dwelleth with you, and shall be in you* (John 14:16, 17).
- *For John truly baptized with water; but ye shall be baptized with the Holy Ghost not many days hence* (Acts 1:5).

The Prophecy of the Outpouring Began to Be Fulfilled With Visible, Audible Evidence

The Holy Ghost was first poured out on disciples and apostles on the Jewish feast day of Pentecost.

- *And when the day of Pentecost was fully come, they were all with one accord in one place. And suddenly there came a sound from heaven as of a rushing mighty wind, and it filled all the house where they were sitting. And there appeared unto them cloven tongues like as of fire, and it sat upon each of them. And they were all filled with the Holy Ghost, and began to speak with other tongues, as the Spirit gave them utterance* (Acts 2:1-4).
- *This Jesus hath God raised up, whereof we all are witnesses. Therefore being by the right hand of God exalted, and having received of the Father the promise of the Holy Ghost, he hath shed forth this, which ye now see and hear* (Acts 2:32, 33).

The second recorded filling of newborn believers occurred at Samaria about one year later.

- *Then laid they their hands on them, and they received the Holy Ghost* (Acts 8:17).

Approximately ten years after the Pentecostal outpouring, the

Holy Ghost fell on the Gentile believers at the house of Cornelius.

- *While Peter yet spake these words, the Holy Ghost fell on all them which heard the word. And they of the circumcision which believed were astonished, as many as came with Peter, because that on the Gentiles also was poured out the gift of the Holy Ghost. For they heard them speak with tongues, and magnify God* (Acts 10:44-46).
- *And as I began to speak, the Holy Ghost fell on them, as on us at the beginning. Then remembered I the word of the Lord, how that he said, John indeed baptized with water; but ye shall be baptized with the Holy Ghost* (Acts 11:15, 16).

Some 25 years after the first outpouring, the Holy Ghost came on some long-time disciples at Ephesus.

- *And when Paul had laid his hands upon them, the Holy Ghost came on them; and they spake with tongues, and prophesied* (Acts 19:6).

Speaking in Tongues Is an Evident Sign to the Unbeliever

Speaking in (new, unknown or other) tongues is a sign to the unbelievers.

- *Wherefore tongues are a sign, not to them that believe, but to them that believe not* (1 Corinthians 14:22a).

Speaking in tongues was foretold by Jesus as a sign which was to follow believers.

- *And these signs shall follow them that believe; In my name shall they cast out devils; they shall speak with new tongues* (Mark 16:17).

Speaking in tongues was foretold by an Old Testament prophet, who prophesied also that it would not be accepted.

- *For with stammering lips and another tongue will he speak to this people. To whom he said, "This is the rest wherewith ye may cause the weary to rest; and this is the refreshing: yet they would not hear"* (Isaiah 28:11, 12).

Paul referred to Isaiah's prophecy that this sign would not be accepted.

- *In the law it is written, with men of other tongues and other lips will I speak unto this people; and yet for all that will they not hear me, saith the Lord* (1 Corinthians 14:21).

Every Believer Should Seek to Be Filled With the Holy Ghost

The believer may receive the baptism of the Holy Ghost as soon as he is saved.

- *Who shall tell thee words, whereby thou and all thy house shall be saved. And as I began to speak, the Holy Ghost fell on them, as on us at the beginning* (Acts 11:14, 15).

The believer may receive the baptism of the Holy Ghost a short time after salvation.

- *Who, when they were come down, prayed for them, that they might receive the Holy Ghost: (for as yet he was fallen upon none of them: only they were baptized in the name of the Lord Jesus.) Then laid they their hands on them, and they received the Holy Ghost* (Acts 8:15-17).

There may be a long interval between salvation and the baptism of the Holy Ghost.

- *He said unto them, "Have ye received the Holy Ghost since ye believed?" And they said unto him, "We have not so much as heard whether there be any Holy Ghost." And he said unto them, "Unto what then were ye baptized?" And they said, "Unto John's baptism." Then said Paul, "John verily baptized with the baptism of repentance, saying unto the people, that they should believe on him which should come after him, that is, on Christ Jesus." When they heard this, they were baptized in the name of the Lord Jesus. And when Paul had laid his hands upon them, the Holy Ghost came on them; and they spake with tongues, and prophesied* (Acts 19:2-6).

The believer may be baptized in water before receiving the baptism of the Holy Ghost.

- *(For as yet he was fallen upon none of them: only they were baptized in the name of the Lord Jesus.) Then laid they their hands on them, and they received the Holy Ghost* (Acts 8:16, 17).

The believer may be baptized in water after receiving the baptism of the Holy Ghost.

- *Can any man forbid water, that these should not be baptized, which have received the Holy Ghost as well as we? And he commanded them to be baptized in the name of the Lord* (Acts 10:47, 48).

The dedicated believer may be refilled with the Holy Ghost from time to time.

- *Then Peter, filled with the Holy Ghost, said unto them...* (Acts 4:8a).
- *And when they prayed, the place was shaken where they were assembled together; and they were all filled with the Holy Ghost, and they spake the word of God with boldness* (Acts 4:31).
- *And the disciples were filled with joy, and with the Holy Ghost* (Acts 13:52).

The believer does not have to be an apostle or a full-time minister to be filled with the Holy Ghost.

- *Then the twelve called the multitude of the disciples unto them, and said, It is not reason that we should leave the word of God, and serve tables. Wherefore, brethren, look ye out among you seven men of honest report, full of the Holy Ghost and wisdom, whom we may appoint over this business. But we will give ourselves continually to prayer, and to the ministry of the word* (Acts 6:2-4).

The Baptism in the Holy Ghost Is Available to All Believers During the Church Age

The Spirit of God was restricted to select spiritual leaders during the Old Testament times.

- *And Moses said unto him, "Enviest thou for my sake? Would God that all the Lord's people were prophets, and that the Lord would put his spirit upon them"* (Numbers 11:29).

But the baptism in the Holy Ghost is promised to all during this dispensation.

- *And it shall come to pass in the last days, saith God, "I will pour out of my Spirit upon all flesh: and your sons and your daughters shall prophesy"* (Acts 2:17a).

The baptism in the Holy Ghost was promised to every believer all down through the church age.

- *Then Peter said unto them, "Repent, and be baptized every one of you in the name of Jesus Christ for the remission of sins, and ye shall receive the gift of the Holy Ghost. For the promise is unto you, and to your children, and to all that are afar off, even as many as the Lord our God shall call"* (Acts 2:38, 39).

The baptism in the Holy Ghost is for those who are obedient.

- *And we are his witnesses of these things; and so is also the Holy Ghost, whom God hath given to them that obey him* (Acts 5:32).

The baptism in the Holy Ghost is for those who pray persistently—who importune.

- *If ye then, being evil, know how to give good gifts unto your children: how much more shall your heavenly Father give the Holy Spirit to them that ask him* (Luke 11:13). (Read Luke 11:5-13.)

The baptism in the Holy Ghost is for those who tarry, who wait on God.

- *And, behold, I send the promise of my Father upon you: but tarry ye in the city of Jerusalem, until ye be endued with power from on high (Luke 24:49). And, being assembled together with them, commanded them that they should not depart from Jerusalem, but wait for the promise of the Father, which, saith he, ye have heard of me* (Acts 1:4).

The Real Purpose of the Baptism in the Holy Ghost Is to Empower the Believer to Tell the Story of Jesus to the Lost

The Holy Ghost gives the believer power to become an effective witness for Christ.

- *But ye shall receive power, after that the Holy Ghost is come upon you: and ye shall be witnesses unto me . . . unto the uttermost part of the earth* (Acts 1:8).

The believer whose power and boldness to witness has waned, or whose power and boldness need to be increased, may be refilled with the Holy Ghost

- *And when they* [*this they includes Peter and John and other very consecrated disciples*] *had prayed, the place was shaken where they were assembled together; and they were all filled with the Holy Ghost, and they spake the word of God with boldness* (Acts 4:31).

On Speaking in Tongues

The term *speaking in tongues* (new, unknown, other or divers kinds of) is used in the Bible in reference to:

1. The baptism or receiving of the Holy Spirit (Acts 2:4; 10:46; 19:6)
2. The last two of the nine gifts of the Holy Spirit

   (1 Corinthians 12:8-10); and,
3. Individual religious devotions (1 Corinthians 14:14, 15 and 28b).

In each case the term is used in connection with a spiritual manifestation: "And they were all filled with the Holy Ghost, and began to speak with other tongues, as the spirit gave them utterance" (Acts 2:4); and "But the manifestation of the spirit is given to every man to profit withal" (1 Corinthians 12:7); and (the emphasis here is apparently on the man's spirit) "For he that speaketh in an unknown tongue speaketh not unto men, but unto God: for no man understandeth him; howbeit in the spirit he speaketh mysteries . . . For if I pray in an unknown tongue, my spirit prayeth" (1 Corinthians 14:2 and verse 14a).

It is acknowledged that there is a difference in purpose between speaking in tongues as an indication of one of the supernatural gifts of the Spirit and speaking in tongues as an initial evidence of the baptism of the Holy Ghost—and between these two and the use of unknown tongues as a means of communicating with God in prayer, praise, and singing. However, since the manifestation is, in appearance, either exactly the same, or quite similar in all of these cases, no great effort is made in this appendix to show a clear-cut distinction among the various purposes for speaking in tongues.

In the 14th chapter of 1 Corinthians, the apostle Paul, who spoke with tongues: "I thank my God, I speak with tongues more than ye all" (verse 18), counsels the Corinthian church regarding the wise use of this spiritual gift. He gives separate instructions for its use (in the church, i.e., when speaking to the Christian assembly (verse 19), and for its use in personal devotions (verses 14, 15, and 28) outside the regular instructional part of the service or at home.

Paul states that one who prophesies in or to the Christian assembly edifies the whole church, whereas "he that speaketh in an unknown tongue" edifies only himself (verse 4). The apostle indicates that one who prophesies is greater than one who speaks with tongues unless the latter can also interpret in order that the church may be edified (verse 5). He goes so far as to say that one should not speak to the church assembly in tongues when there is no interpreter present (verse 28). To speak thus in tongues to the brethren in an assembly is, according to Paul, profitless (verse 6), is the same as giving an indistinct sound on a musical instrument (verse 7), is like an uncertain bugle command during battle (verse 8), is of no more value than speaking into the air (verse 9), is meaningless to the hearer (verses 11 and 16), is not instructive (verse 19), and will cause the unlearned or unbelievers to think that those whom they hear are mad (verse 23).

Speaking in tongues to the assembly of brethren where there is an interpreter, however, is equal to the gift of prophecy (verse 5), is edifying to the church (verses 5, 12, 13, and 26), and should follow this pattern: "If any man speak in an unknown tongue, let it be by two, or at the most by three, and that by course; and let one interpret" (verse 27). Paul believes that this pattern can be followed because "the spirits of the prophets are subject to the prophets" (verse 32); and he advises to "Let all things be done decently and in order" (verse 40). Paul places no great limitations, however, on the manifestation of this gift when the believer is alone and seeking spiritual edification: "He that speaketh in an unknown tongue edifieth himself" (verse 4); when the believer is in prayer and in praiseful singing: "For if I pray in an unknown tongue, my spirit prayeth, but my understanding is unfruitful. What is it then I will pray with the spirit . . . I will sing with the spirit" (verses 14, 15); when the believer is in church (assembly) and there is an interpreter present (verse 27); and even when the believer is in church where there is no interpreter provided he speaks inaudibly: "But if there be no interpreter, let him keep silence in the church; and let him speak to himself, and to God" (verse 28).

The apostle Paul comprehended the spiritual significance of speaking in tongues: "For he that speaketh in an unknown tongue speaketh not unto men, but unto God: for no man understandeth him; howbeit, in the spirit he speaketh mysteries" (verse 2), he desired that all Christians possess this gift: "I would that ye all spake with tongues" (verse 5); he possessed the gift himself: "I thank my God, I speak with tongues more than ye all" (verse 18); he prayed and sang in an unknown tongue (verses 14, 15); he knew that speaking in tongues was a prophesied sign from the Lord (verses 21, 22); he realized that the world would not accept it: "And yet for all that will they not hear me, saith the Lord" (verse 21); and he understood that Christians were to be permitted to speak with tongues: "Wherefore, brethren, covet to prophesy, and forbid not to speak with tongues" (verse 39). Paul also knew that tongues would cease and told us when: Tongues will cease when prophecies fail, when knowledge vanishes away, and "when that which is perfect is come" (1 Corinthians 13:8-10).

Lesson 5: How to Handle Temptation and Sin

(Subjects: Temptation, Sin, Obedience)

> *The trouble with trouble is that it usually starts out as a whole lot of fun (Unknown).*
>
> *I can resist anything except temptation* (Oscar Wilde).

Memory Verse for This Lesson

> *No temptation has seized you except what is common to man. And God is faithful; he will not let you be tempted beyond what you can bear. But when you are tempted, he will also provide a way out so that you can stand up under it* (1 Corinthians 10:13).

Though a plane soars through the sky, gravity constantly pulls down on the plane. In a similar way, the obedient Christian life is filled with joy; nevertheless, temptation and sin constantly seek to pull us down. Why does this happen?

Simply put, there is a constant struggle between the Spirit and the flesh. "For the sinful nature [the flesh] desires what is contrary to the Spirit, and the Spirit what is contrary to the sinful nature. They are in conflict with each other, so that you do not do what you want" (Galatians 5:17).

How can we have victory over our temptations and forgiveness for our sins? Let's begin by exploring the difference between temptation and sin.

Where Is the Line That Separates Temptation and Sin?

Little Johnny drew a line in the sand and said to his brother, "You'd better not cross that line or I'll beat you up!"

Little Jimmy, up to the dare, immediately and defiantly stepped across the line and folded his arms across his chest as if in triumph. His brother Johnny paused hesitantly for a moment, drew another line in the sand, and repeated, "You'd better not cross that line or I'll beat you up!"

Where is the fuzzy line that separates temptation from sin? Is it a line etched in stone or in shifting sand? Is it one that we can continue to redraw when we don't like the immediate results? What is the difference between a temptation and an actual sin?

Many of us don't clearly understand the difference between temptation and sin, so we often feel like we are treading water without knowing where the bottom is. We are like the six-foot man who drowned in four feet of water.

Temptation Is Not Sin

The tempting thoughts that enter our minds are not sins in and of themselves. We ask ourselves, *How could I be a true Christian, and still have these thoughts? I must not have genuine faith.* But there are two things we must keep in mind:

1. We have a nature within us that is contrary to God: "For in my inner being I delight in God's law; but I see another law at work in the members of my body, waging war against the law of my mind and making me a prisoner of the law of sin at work within my members. What a wretched man I am! Who will rescue me from this body of death?" (Romans 7:22-24). As long as we are on this earth, we are tied to a body with its own agenda.
2. We are assaulted from the outside by spiritual beings as well: "For our struggle is not against flesh and blood, but against the rulers, against the authorities, against the powers of this dark world and against the spiritual forces of evil in the heavenly realms" (Ephesians 6:12).

Such attacks are like the vulgar language of the man sitting next to us at a restaurant. We hear them both, but we don't control whether or not we hear them. It is our voluntary response to the involuntary stimulus that makes the difference.

Temptation is the first step along a continuum that will lead to sin if we do not turn away. We often put ourselves into compromising situations so that our minds are predisposed to tempting thoughts. The best policy is to avoid situations that you know will tempt, entice, and lure you to sin.

When Temptation Crosses the Line

What is the difference between a temptation and an actual sin? The best example is sex. Generally, since men are physically attracted to women, when does mental attraction become sin? Is there some definable threshold over which we cross from mere temptation to actual sin?

When our *normal* observations become *abnormal* preoccupations, then we have crossed the line. Dr. R. C. Sproul, in his book *Pleasing God,* noted these thoughts:

> *Lust is not noticing that a woman is sexually attractive. Lust is born when we turn a simple awareness into a preoccupied fantasy. When we invite sexual thoughts into our minds and nurture them, we have passed from simple awareness into lust [sin]. Luther put it this way: "We cannot help it if birds fly over our heads. It is another thing if we invite them to build nests in our hair".*[1]

A friend said it this way, "Temptation is sexual attraction to a beautiful woman. Sin is walking around the block for another look." As Jesus himself said, "But I tell you that anyone who looks at a woman *lustfully* has already committed adultery with her in his heart" (Matthew 5:28).

Webster's Dictionary says that to be tempted is to be "enticed to commit an unwise or immoral act." Temptation is to be enticed; sin is to become entangled.

When our chest swells in pride for a job well done, we feel better about ourselves as human beings. When does feeling good about our accomplishments become sin? When we begin to compare our accomplishments to other men and begin to elevate ourselves above others, we have crossed over the line.

Dwight L. Moody, the great 19th century evangelist, said, "When Christians find themselves exposed to temptation they should pray to God to uphold them, and when they are tempted they should not be discouraged. It is not a sin to be tempted; the sin is to fall into temptation."

WHERE DOES TEMPTATION COME FROM?

Answer the following questions by looking up the indicated verses and putting the answer in your own words.

Who is the tempter? (Matthew 4:1-3).

___

Who is never the tempter? (James 1:13).

___

What is our part in temptation? (James 1:14).

___

Everyone is tempted to sin. Look up 1 John 2:16. What are the three ways in which we are tempted?

1. ___
2. ___
3. ___

The Bible also promises victory over our temptations. Look up 1 Corinthians 10:13 (this lesson's memory verse) and answer the following questions:

1. Are there any unique temptations that only you have had?

   ___

2. How far will God let you be tempted?

____

3. What does the Bible promise to provide you when tempted?

____

4. Why does God provide a way out?

____

Where Does Sin Come From?

Sin is a human failure done in rebellion against God and His Word. Sin results from trusting in self, not God. Sin is where God is not. It is a *choice*. We can choose to live by the Spirit and accept God's provision to have victory over our temptations. Or we can choose to live by the flesh (our "own evil desire" [James 1:14]) and be dragged away and enticed.

Everyone sins. Inevitably, we can all be overcome and give way to temptation. According to 1 John 1:9, what is the provision God has made for us when we succumb to temptation and sin?

____

Allowed to go far enough, sin can destroy our relationship with God.[2] Wise is the man who daily goes to God in self-examination, confessing and repenting of his sins. Consider making this prayer of David a regular part of your daily spiritual disciplines:

> *Search me, O God, and know my heart; test me and know my anxious thoughts. See if there is any offensive way in me, and lead me in the way everlasting* (Psalm 139:23, 24).

A Life of Obedience

Bill Bright wisely said, "There are no happy disobedient Christians. Conversely, there are no unhappy obedient Christians."

By living a life of obedience we will increasingly exhibit the fruit of the Spirit—love, joy, peace, patience, kindness, goodness, faithfulness, gentleness, and self-control. Jesus said, "If you love me, you will obey what I command" (John 14:15). Obedience is how we demonstrate our love for Jesus in a tangible way.

This obedience is not generated from our own willpower. Rather, the obedient life is simply letting Christ in you live His life through you by the power of the Holy Spirit.

According to the following passages, what are some practical ways to avoid temptation and sin?

1 Corinthians 6:18

___

Ephesians 4:26, 27

___

2 Timothy 2:16

___

2 Timothy 2:22

___

James 4:7

___

Summary of Key Points

- Simply put, there is a constant struggle between the Spirit and the flesh.
- It is our voluntary response to the involuntary stimulus that makes the difference.
- Sin is when *normal* observations become *abnormal* preoccupations.
- Temptation is to be *enticed,* sin is to become *entangled.*
- We are tempted by *the devil, the flesh, and the world.*

- Sin is a human failure done in rebellion against God and His Word.
- Sin is a *choice.*
- If we confess our sins God will forgive our sins (1 John 1:9).
- Sin can destroy our relationship with God.
- "There are no happy disobedient Christians."
- The obedient life is simply letting Christ in you live His life through you by the power of the Holy Spirit.

A Final Reflection

Have you ever thought about why we sin? Sin produces immediate pleasure. It gives a physical, spiritual and emotional rush. We do not sin out of obligation. We sin because we believe that it will provide a pleasure that is superior to the pleasure of obedience to God. The power of temptation rests on a deceptive promise that sin will bring more satisfaction than living for God. The Word of God calls this promise the deceitfulness of sin or the deceitful lusts.

We will only win the battle of temptation as we enjoy God. The secret to conquering sin is satisfaction in God. The Holy Spirit is setting forth the beauty of God in Jesus Christ so that we might become enticed by a holy affection whose power rivals the power of our sin (Mike Bickle, *The Pleasures of Loving God,* p. 125).

[1] R. C. Sproul, *Pleasing God,* (Wheaton: Tyndale House Publishers, Inc., 1988), p. 79.

[2] There is nothing "un-Protestant" about belief in the possible falling away of the believer after salvation. "He who does what is sinful is of the devil, because the devil has been sinning from the beginning" (1 John 3:8a, also see Lesson 3). "NOT every deadly sin willingly committed after Baptism is sin against the Holy Ghost, and unpardonable. Wherefore the grant of repentance is not to be denied to such as fall into sin after Baptism. After we have received the Holy Ghost, we may depart from grace given and fall into sin, and by the grace of God we may arise again and amend our lives. And therefore they are to be condemned, which say they can no more sin as long as they live here, or deny the place of forgiveness to such as truly repent" (Article of Religion XVI, see Lesson 9).

Lesson 6: How to Be a Successful Husband and Father

(Subjects: Marriage, Family)

> *Let the wife make the husband glad to come home, and let him make her sorry to see him leave (*Martin Luther).
>
> *My child arrived just the other day; he came to the world in the usual way. But there were planes to catch and bills to pay; he learned to walk while I was away (Cat's in the Cradle,* Sandy and Harry Chapin).

Memory Verses for This Lesson

> *Husbands, love your wives and do not be harsh with them* (Colossians 3:19).
>
> *Fathers, do not exasperate your children; instead, bring them up in the training and instruction of the Lord* (Ephesians 6:4).

Marriage: How to Be a Successful Husband

In *Rocky,* voted best movie of 1976, the central character, Rocky, is a dull-witted neighborhood pug who operates just beyond the fringe of the real world. He falls in love with Adrian, a pale, homely pet store clerk who repeatedly deflects his romantic interest. Finally, Adrian's brother Paulie, Rocky's friend, virtually forces them together and, at long last, Adrian returns Rocky's affections.

Later, Paulie is astonished that his sister and Rocky really got together and asks Rocky, "How are you getting along together? What's the story? What's happening? You really like her?"

"Sure I like her."

"I don't see it. What's the attraction?"

"I don't know. I guess it fills in gaps."

"What's gaps?"

"I don't know—gaps. She's got gaps. I've got gaps. Together we fill gaps."

God gives each of us gaps. Sometimes these gaps are *weaknesses,* other times they are *unmet needs.* A wife's greatest gap is the need to be loved, and a husband's greatest gap is the need to be respected. Let's discuss the needs of a successful marriage.

A Wife's Greatest Need

Have you ever wondered why wives don't need to be reminded to love their husbands? That's because after the fall of Adam and Eve, God said to the woman, "Your desire will be for your husband, and he will rule over you" (Genesis 3:16). God gives wives the desire to love their husbands, and to be fulfilled she needs to feel loved, cherished, and nurtured by her husband.

God did not leave fulfilling this need to chance. Instead, He gave husbands an instruction to fill the needs of their wives. "However, each one of you also must love his wife as he loves himself..." (Ephesians 5:33).

Have you ever wondered why husbands *do* have to be reminded to love their wives? That's because the greatest need of *men* (as distinguished from *husbands)* is to be significant. Men want to have an impact, to make a contribution, to do something important. God gave men the natural inclination to be task oriented. They usually fulfill this need in their work, not their marriage. Do you need to make any changes to fulfill your Biblical responsibility to your wife? If so, what will you do?

A Husband's Greatest Need

While wives need to be loved, a husband's greatest gap is the need to be respected by his wife. God did not leave fulfilling this need to chance, either. Instead, in the last half of Ephesians 5:33, He gave wives an instruction to fill the need of their husbands, " ... and the wife must respect her husband."

Nothing brightens the inner spirit of a man than to be respected by his wife. Conversely, nothing dims the lights of a marriage quicker than for the husband to not love his wife.

The Role of the Wife

What is the principal role of the wife in marriage according to Ephesians 5:22?

____

What does it mean to *submit?* The Greek word *submit* translates from Greek into English as "to subordinate, to obey, or to submit one's self unto." The goal of this instruction is not to reduce women to servants and doormats, but to provide an authority structure in the marriage.

Remember what was said to the woman in Genesis 3:16, "Your desire will be for your husband, *and he will rule over you"* (emphasis added). Marriage is an institution established by God that, like all other institutions, needs an authority structure.

What happens when the wife does not submit? The opposite of *submission* is *resistance.* When the wife resists the established authority structure the result is strife, disorder, and sometimes even chaos.

Figure 1 shows a continuum between submitting and resisting. Where is your wife on the continuum? If she is not a submitting wife, how have your attitudes and actions contributed to her stance?

Figure 1

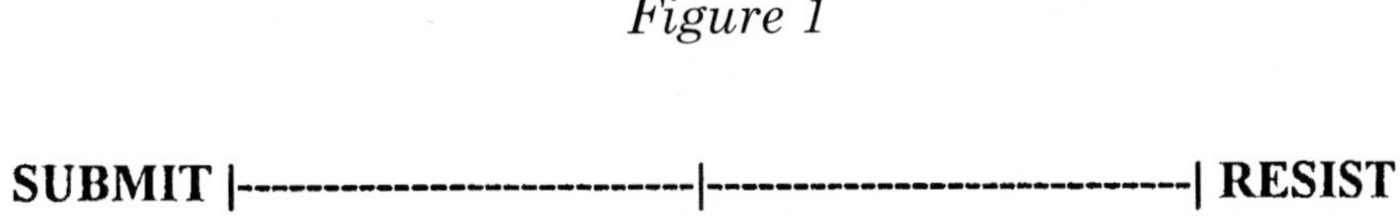

The Role of the Husband

What is the principal role of the husband in marriage according to Ephesians 5:25?

What does it mean to *love?* The Greek word for how men are to love their wives is the same word God used to describe His own love for the world. "For God so *loved* the world that he gave his one and only Son" (John 3:16). It's also the same kind of love we are to have for God. *"Love* the Lord your God with all your heart and with all your soul and with all your mind" (Matthew 22:37).

What kind of love is this? The kind of love Scripture directs us to is *volitional* love rather than *emotional* love. Scriptural love is *agape* love, which means to love in a moral sense; it is a deliberate act of the *will* as a matter of principle, duty, and propriety. In short, Biblical love is a *decision,* not *a feeling.*

What happens when the husband does not love his wife? The opposite of *love* is *hate.* Hate in its worst form goes by the name of indifference. We can tell ourselves that we don't hate our wives, but if we don't care the difference is academic.

Figure 2 shows another continuum, this time for husbands. Where would you place the "X" for yourself? What is a practical step you can take this week (e.g., flowers, a date, a phone call from work) to demonstrate your Biblical responsibility to love your wife?

Figure 2

LOVE |------------------------|--------------------------| **HATE**

If a wife can submit or resist, and if a husband can love or hate, then how many marriage combinations can we come up with? The answer is four.

1. Love and Submit
2. Hate and Submit
3. Love and Resist
4. Hate and Resist

Which combination best describes your marriage at the present time, and why? What changes could you make that would improve your marriage?

We all have gaps—unmet needs and weaknesses. These are the gaps that God has allowed in our lives. God gives people with gaps to people with gaps to fill each other's gaps. Be sure to fill your wife's gaps.

Other Roles of the Husband

Look up the following verses and write down the other Biblical roles of a husband:

Colossians 3:19

---

1 Timothy 5:8

---

1 Peter 3:7

The Mutuality of Marriage

Although husbands and wives have different roles, and although the Bible provides a distinct authority structure for marriage, the Bible also calls for a mutual dependence. What should you do differently in your own marriage based upon Ephesians 5:21 and 1 Corinthians 11:11?

What are the ways marriages get into trouble? List at least five.

1. ______________________________

2. ______________________________

3. ______________________________

4. ______________________________

5. ______________________________

In which of these areas is your marriage weakest? What are three practical steps you can take this week to strengthen your marriage?

1. ______________________________

2. ______________________________

3. ______________________________

Application

Are you less than happily married? Perhaps you are not unhappy, but you sense you are missing out on the best that marriage can offer. Have your wife review this material, and then spend some time together answering the 16 questions in Appendix A at the end of this section titled, "Questions to Discuss With Your Spouse." Make a habit of spending time together every day building a personal relationship—20 minutes would be good. You may just become best friends.

Family: How to Be a Successful Father

The Bible is replete with examples of fathers who failed, but is in short supply of successes. King David, for example, despite all his strengths, was a weak father.

David tried to delegate his role as father with disastrous results. "Jehiel son of Hacmoni took care of the king's sons" (1 Chronicles 27:32b). And what was the result? A brood of rebellious sons.

His son Amnon raped his own sister Tamar. Then his son Absalom took revenge and had Amnon murdered. Later, his son Adonijah planned a coup and tried to appoint himself king. The Bible reports, "His father had never interfered with him by asking, 'Why do you behave as you do?'" (1 Kings 1:6).

Fatherhood cannot be delegated. It is a task that only you can do.

The Needs of a Child

Larry Crabb, Christian psychologist, says that children need to know two things:

1. Yes, my parents love me.
2. No, I can't have my own way.

Why is that? The answer is found in the Bible. The Bible tells us that children are not wise but foolish. "Folly is bound up in the heart of a child ..." (Proverbs 22:15). Our children—not wise, but foolish—want to have their own way. It is the father's responsibility to instruct them in the ways of the Lord, while expressing unconditional love in the process. Syrupy permissiveness will only appeal to the foolishness bound up in their hearts.

There are four possible combinations of Larry Crabb's two points. Write down the probable outcome for each combination listed:

1. Yes, my parents love me and, no, I can't have my own way.

____

2. No, my parents don't love me and, no, I can't have my own way.

3. Yes, my parents love me and, yes, I can have my own way.

4. No, my parents don't love me and yes, I can have my own way.

Which of these four scenarios best describes your home, and why? What changes would improve your home?

What does the Bible tell us children need from each of the following verses?

Proverbs 22:15

Ephesians 6:4

Colossians 3:21

Disciplining our children is important. When fathers err in their disciplining, do you think they tend to *over* discipline or *under* discipline? How about you?

The Bible contains very few direct instructions to fathers. Why do you think so much emphasis is placed upon the father's exasperating and embittering of his children?

What are some ways fathers discourage rather than encourage their children?

1. ______________________________

2. ______________________________

3. ______________________________

4. ______________________________

5. ______________________________

Which of these do you do? What practical steps can you take to change direction?

____

The Responsibilities of a Father

We have looked at what our children need. Now let us turn our attention to our responsibilities as fathers. Look up the following verses and record the responsibilities the Bible gives to fathers.

"Folly is bound up in the heart of a child, but the rod of discipline will drive it far from him" (Proverbs 22:15).

Deuteronomy 6:6-9

____

Proverbs 22:6

____

Proverbs 22:15

____

Ephesians 6:4

____

1 Timothy 5:8

____

Colossians 3:21

Practical Suggestions for Being a Successful Father

1. *Pray for your children.* You may be the only person in the entire world willing to pray for your children on a regular basis. Appendix B provides a suggested list of topics. You may find some adaptation of this list useful.
2. *Give your children a heart for God.* The greatest heritage you can give your child is a heart for God. One practical way to achieve this is to encourage your children to have daily devotions. Let them pick out a devotional book and involve yourself daily in their time with God.
3. *Love their mother.* It's been said, "The greatest gift a father can give to his children is to love their mother." Dr. Frank Minirth of the famous Minirth-Meier Clinic says, "The most important, the number one thing in a child's life is for you to love your wife and raise your kids as a team. Kids are incredibly sensitive to that." Their security stands on the foundation of love.
4. *Spend time with your children.* Time is everything to a relationship. Give time to whom time is due. No amount of success at the office can compensate for failure at home. Most men, in the wake of their ambition, leave a trail of broken relationships. If you don't have enough time for your family, you can be 100 percent certain you are not following God's will for your life. Be there for their school events, take them on special outings, let them change a flat tire—even though it will take twice as long. Make it a priority. A child can accidentally turn out wrong, but turning out right is no accident. No matter how unhappy your life may be now, it does not compare to how unhappy you will be if your children are unhappy later.
5. *Teach your children about money.* Insist that they form the habit from their earliest days of saving 10 percent and tithing 10 percent of their allowances and earnings. This may seem like an abstract idea to your children, but it is likely they will

have to provide for their own "social security."

6. *Offer your children protection from the world.* Protection is different than insulation. There are no secrets anymore. The best protection is to openly discuss everything with your children. Whatever you do, don't leave them to discover their sexuality on their own. When men err, they often tend to under-protect, not overprotect, somehow believing their children to be as mature as they say they are. Help them overcome peer pressure. A 15-year-old girl said to her parents, "Please, tell me I'm not allowed to ride in the car when Robin is driving." The best antidote for peer pressure is parent pressure. Your home should be a haven of rest from the troubles of the world. Overlook offenses when you can. Let the little ones go. Keep the temperature cool.
7. *Teach your children Biblical values and beliefs.* In computers, the default value is the value used by the computer unless the user alters it to use another specified value. If we do not teach our children Biblical values and beliefs, they will assume the default values of their culture. What are the default values of our culture in marriage? education? spiritual convictions? music? books? television? sex? substances? saving? tithing? integrity? work ethic? authority? truth? Are these the values and beliefs you want for your children? Folly is bound up in the heart of a child. The duty of fathers is to train up their children, to teach, to instruct, to encourage, to discipline. If you do not build their value system and belief system, someone else will. Who would that be in your case? Remember that values are often caught, not taught. You have to live out what you say.
8. *Prepare your children for life.* Many fathers never discuss with their children what their major life decisions will be. What are the critical factors to make sure those decisions are in God's will? These include who to marry, where to go to college, what kind of career to pursue, and what kind of friends to choose. There are many daily decisions for which fathers should prepare their children. For example, how to respond to temptations, how to resolve conflict, and how to establish

priorities and manage time. Why not make a list of the most important lessons you want to teach your children and review it with them—perhaps one item per night during the dinner meal. Encourage them to come to you with their questions.

Appendix A: Solving Our Relationship Problems

Questions to discuss with your spouse: (Spend 20 minutes together daily for 30 days—form a habit.)

1. What are three to five things about me that you really like?
2. What are two things I do which you wish I would stop doing or change?
3. Where are you on your spiritual pilgrimage?
4. What do you think is the purpose of your life?
5. What is something we could do together in our spare time?
6. What is a trip you've always dreamed of taking?
7. What are your greatest regrets about your life?
8. What has been your biggest disappointment?
9. How do you feel about how the children are turning (have turned) out?
10. If you could change any one thing about your life, what would it be?
11. If you had no one else to answer to, what would you like to be doing in five years? Ten years? In retirement?
12. What is one tangible way I can better express my love for you?
13. Each put an "X" where you think you are and where your partner is:

Men: Figure 1

LOVE |------------------------|-------------------------| HATE

Women: Figure 2

SUBMIT |--------------------------|----------------------------| RESIST

Discuss why your answers are different. Discuss each other's willingness to change.

14. Which of the four types of marriages do we have?
15. What practical steps could I / you take to have a "love and submit" marriage?
16. Husband: Read 1 Corinthians 13 to your wife out loud. Confess to her the areas where you have failed and ask her forgiveness. Wife: Repeat.

Appendix B: Children: How to Avoid Regrets

Pray for your children for the following:

- A saving faith (thanksgiving if already Christian)
- A growing faith
- An independent faith (as they grow up)
- To be strong and healthy in mind, body and spirit
- A sense of destiny (purpose)
- A desire for integrity
- A call to excellence
- To understand the ministry God has for them
- That I will set aside times to spend with them
- To acquire wisdom
- Protection from drugs, alcohol, premarital sex, AIDS and other STD's
- The mate God has for them (alive somewhere, needing prayer)
- Glorify the Lord in everything

Can you think of anything in the entire world more important than for your children to place faith in Jesus Christ and to experience God's wonderful plan for their lives? Through prayer, and the model of your own life, you can have confidence that, by God's grace, they will.

No man would be unwilling to die for his children. How much more important it is to live for them.

A Final Reflection

A number of years ago, Dr. Robert Schuller was on a whirlwind book promotion tour, visiting eight cities in four days. It was an exhausting schedule in addition to the normal duties that Dr. Schuller had on his shoulders as pastor of a large church. As he was going over his schedule with his secretary for his return home, she reminded him that he was scheduled to have lunch with the winner of a charity raffle. Tickets had been raffled for a lunch with Dr. Schuller. Schuller was suddenly sobered when he found out the winner of the raffle, for he happened to know that the $500 the person bid to have lunch with him represented that person's entire life savings. How did he know that? The person who was willing to spend $500 to have lunch with Dr. Schuller was his own teenage daughter (Steve Farrar, *Standing Tall,* p. 224).

Lesson 7: How to Be Financially Successful

(Subjects: Work, Ethics, Money, Stewardship, Priorities)

> *Anytime someone says it's not the money but the principle of the thing—it's the money* (Elbert Hubbard).
>
> *No one ever said on their deathbed, "I wish I had spent more time with my business"* (Lee Iacocca).
>
> *Always do the right thing. This will gratify some people and astonish the rest* (Mark Twain).

Memory Verse for This Lesson

> *Do you see a man skilled in his work? He will serve before kings; he will not serve before obscure men* (Proverbs 22:29).

A man who works 40 hours a week for 40 years with a two-week annual vacation will spend 80,000 hours on the job. During those same 40 years, assuming he sleeps eight hours each night, he will be awake 233,000 hours. So, a man will spend about one-third of his waking hours at work.

It is quite remarkable that though we spend so much time at our careers, so many struggle with finding fulfillment and a sense of purpose in their work. You do not need to be in ministry to have meaningful work. Every honest vocation has intrinsic value and is ordained by God. Teaching the Bible in a college is no higher calling than being a businessman or a lawyer or a plumber. What really matters is what Gods calls you to do—it's all a matter of calling.

It is discouraging to see the prevalence of ethical failures in the work world. It is distressing to see the number of men who, for whatever reasons, do not achieve financial independence.

What do we all hope to accomplish through our careers? There are three primary desired end results in particular which are capstones of a successful career:

1. A Good Reputation
2. A Measure of Prosperity
3. A Balanced Life.

These three, by degrees, swallow up all the dreams, desires, goals, ambitions, and motives of Christian men. They represent what a successful businessman hopes to have at the end of his career to show for his labors.

How do we get there? Easily the most useful and practical book of the Bible for men in the marketplace is Proverbs. The man who would become wise should read and reread this book of 31 chapters.

Proverbs and other parts of the Bible suggest a number of key principles to achieve the three capstones mentioned. Let's explore nine of them together.

A Good Reputation

One measure of a successful career is to end up with an unsullied reputation.

Read Proverbs 22:1. What is the gist of this passage?

The Bible places a premium on a good name. Do you agree? How much attention have you given to your name? Are you satisfied, and if not, what would you do differently?

Dealing with absolute integrity, demonstrating humility, and performing your work with excellence, makes a good name. Let's amplify these points briefly.

1. Cling to Integrity

George Burns once said, "The most important thing in acting is honesty. If you can fake that, you've got it made."

What is integrity?

___

A cab driver offered a blank receipt. "You fill it in however you want," he said.

"No, that's okay. You see, I'm a Christian. That wouldn't be right."

After a long, blank stare, the Christian just shrugged his shoulders and said, "Okay, buddy, whatever you say."

Christian integrity is a one-to-one correlation between your Bible, your belief, and your behavior. Christian integrity means clinging to your honor in every detail of life, no matter how minute or seemingly inconsequential. Anyone can do the big things right, but it's the little things that count.

How does God view dishonesty according to Proverbs 11:1?

___

Read Luke 16:10-12. What happens to honest, trustworthy men?

___

What happens to dishonest, untrustworthy men?

___

What changes would you like to make in this area?

___

According to Colossians 3:22, what is the responsibility of a slave (employee) to his master (employer)?

___

How should employees work according to Colossians 3:22?

___

How are employers to treat their employees according to Colossians 4:1?

___

How important is integrity to you? Where does your behavior not match your belief?

---

2. Be Humble

From the following verses, what is the fate of the proud?

Proverbs 16:18

Proverbs 18:12

What is the fate of the humble?

Proverbs 18:12

James 4:6

Have you been a humble man or a proud man? What changes could you make to be more humble?

---

3. Pursue Excellence

Dr. Francis Schaeffer used to say, "If you do your work well, you will have a chance to speak." Unless we perform our work with excellence, the world will scoff at us and, when we speak, they will not listen.

What is the future for the man who is skilled in his work according to Proverbs 22:29?

A MEASURE OF PROSPERITY

According to the Social Security Administration, at the age of 65 only 2 percent of Americans are financially independent, 30 percent depend on charities, 23 percent must continue to work, and 45 percent are dependent upon relatives. Additionally, 85 of 100 Americans have less than $250 when they reach age 65. According to Devney's Economic Tables, fewer men are worth $100 at age 68 than they were at age 18—after 50 years of hard work![1]

Pity the man who at the end of his life does not have the money to retire—or the time to enjoy it. Every man would do well to consider developing a plan to attain financial independence. What Biblical principles apply?

We attain a measure of prosperity when we save money, share money, and don't go into *debt*. Let's review these three ideas.

4. Save Money

The aforementioned statistics lead us to conclude that more people "under" accumulate than "over" accumulate.

Is it Christian to save money for your future when people all around you have desperate needs? Answer after reading Proverbs 21:20.

What is the Bible's perspective on get-rich-quick and high-risk schemes according to Proverbs 13:11?

The singular key to accumulating capital is to spend less than you earn. What steps, if any, would you need to take to become a net saver? Will you?

According to Proverbs 27:23, 24, why should we look after our assets?

---

5. Share Money

Does it strike you odd that one way to attain prosperity is to actually give money away?

The concept that sharing our wealth enriches us is a uniquely Christian one. It is a reflection of heavenly wealth, which is infinite because it is God's, and which is greater when shared than when hoarded. The Italian poet Dante put it this way in his *Divine Comedy*:

> It is because you focus on the prize
> of worldly goods, which every sharing lessens
> that Envy pumps the bellows for your sighs.
>
> But if, in true love for the Highest Sphere (heaven),
> your longing would be turned upward, then your hearts
> would never be consumed by such a fear;
>
> For the more there are who say "ours"—not "mine"—
> by that much is each richer, and the brighter
> within that cloister burns the Love Divine.

While Proverbs 21:20 makes it clear that a wise man provides for his future, it is conversely true that he is responsible to share with others.

There is a great risk to ourselves when we "over"accumulate money. Read Proverbs 21:13. What are the consequences of shutting our ears to the cry of the poor?

What is the counsel of 1 Timothy 6:17-19 to those who have money?

We must each strike the right balance between saving and sharing what God has given to us. One method, which finds favor with many, is to save 10 percent and tithe 10 percent.

What kind of commitment to saving and sharing is realistic for you?

___

6. Don't Go Into Debt

Consumerism—the economic theory that a progressively greater consumption of goods is beneficial—depends on a constant sparking of our desires to buy things. We can accumulate things two ways: *income* and *debt.* Debt is the opposite of savings. Men either earn interest or pay interest.

Debt enables men to pretend to be somebody else—for a while. Proverbs 13:7 says, "One man pretends to be rich, yet has nothing."

The Bible discourages debt and encourages savings. What does Romans 13:8 say about what we should owe?

___

What does Proverbs 22:7 tell us about borrowers?

___

How has debt been a noose around your neck? What steps could you take to reduce or eliminate your debts? Would you be willing to trade the stress of your debts for a more modest lifestyle?

___

A faithful steward is one who follows God's principles for saving, sharing, and debt. List one step you will take in each area to become more faithful:

- Saving:

  ___

- Sharing:

____

- Debt:

____

A Balanced Life

Isn't a successful businessman really someone who is successful at life, not just work? A balanced life results when we learn to be content, live by Biblical priorities, and submit to God. Let's look closer at these.

7. Learn to Be Content

Gandhi once said, "There is more to life than increasing its speed." The apostle Paul rejoiced because he learned the secret of contentment in all circumstances (see Philippians 4:11, 12).

What is the central thought in each of the following verses?

- 1 Timothy 6:6

____

- 1 Timothy 6:7

____

- 1 Timothy 6:8

____

The idea of contentment is not to force on Christian men a resigned acceptance of their current state. The problem of discontent is the same as poverty. Poverty is the state of not having or earning enough. If there is never an *enough,* one will always be poor, no matter how wealthy one becomes. It is the same with contentment. We can aspire to better ourselves but, if we are never content, moving up will be an exercise in futility because we will never be happy and there will never be enough. Frequently we will find ourselves squandering God's blessings. As one person said, "You can't outgive God, but you can outspend Him!"

Are you a content person? Why or why not?

____

8. Live by Biblical Priorities

Work is important. Work provides income, an outlet for our energies, and a means to find significance. But too much work leads to stress and broken relationships. At the end of their lives, most men measure their success in people and relationships rather than in money and possessions. No amount of success at the office will compensate for failure at home. Many men, in pursuit of their ambitions, leave a trail of broken relationships. Relationship pain is a pain that never goes away. What counsel does Proverbs 23:24, 25 offer?

____

1 Thessalonians 4:11, 12 provides sound advice for the man who would live by Biblical priorities. Summarize that advice.

____

What are the other priorities in your life? List them in order of importance.

1. ____

2. ____

3. ____

4. ____

5. ____

6. ______________________________

Put an "*" next to the ones you have been neglecting because of your work. What changes come to mind?

9. Submit to God's Sovereign Plan

The man who yields his plans to the sovereign will and plan of God will find a peace that eludes the man who resists the Lord.

God has a will for your life. He works out everything in conformity to the purpose of His will. God is sovereign, and His will is being, and will be, done. Learn to trust God. Consider the following verses:

> *There is no wisdom, no insight, no plan that can succeed against the LORD* (Proverbs 21:30).
>
> *Many are the plans in a man's heart, but it is the LORD'S purpose that prevails (Proverbs 19:21).*
>
> *In his heart a man plans his course, but the LORD determines his steps* (Proverbs 16:9).
>
> *To man belong the plans of the heart, but from the LORD comes the reply of the tongue. All a man's ways seem innocent to him, but motives are weighed by the LORD. Commit to the LORD whatever you do, and your plans will succeed. The LORD works out everything for his own ends—even the wicked for a day of disaster* (Proverbs 16:1-4).

What are the recurring themes of these verses?

____

What conclusions can you draw from these verses for your own career?

____

A Final Reflection

If you're like most Americans, you're in debt. On the first day of the New Year, after Christmas purchases have all been given away, you may glance at your checking account and be stunned.

You probably didn't realize the extent of your indebtedness, or how it can affect decision making for your immediate financial future. Here are some facts:

- In the United States, the average balance on a credit card is over $7,000.
- The average interest rate is greater than 19 percent.
- The average household has at least ten credit cards.
- Almost half the households in the United States report having problems paying their minimums.
- If you have a credit card balance of $8,000, and you make the monthly payment at 19 percent interest, it will take you 25 years and seven months to pay the debt off. You will pay an extra $15,432 in interest, making your total payout $23,432.

[1] Ron Blue, *Master Your Money (Nashville: Thomas Nelson Publishers,* 1986), p. 13.

Lesson 8: How to Have an Accountable Relationship

(Subject: Accountability)

> *A friend is one to whom one may pour out all the contents of one's heart, chaff and grain together, knowing that the gentlest of hands will take and sift it, keep what is worth keeping, and with a breath of kindness, blow the rest away (Unkown).*
>
> *The kisses of an enemy may be profuse, but faithful are the wounds of a friend* (Proverbs 27:6).

Memory Verse for This Lesson

> *Two are better than one, because they have a good return for their work: If one falls down, his friend can help him up* (Ecclesiastes 4:9, 10a).

The Need for Accountability

Do you know anyone who ever intentionally ruined his life? No normal person ever failed on purpose. Yet, every day thousands of men fail four ways: *morally, financially, spiritually, and relationally.* They declare bankruptcy, file for divorce, steal from their employers, destroy their children's self-confidence, commit adultery, turn their back on God, and deprive their families of time.

What kind of men are most likely to get into trouble? The correct answer is men who don't have anyone to answer to for their lives—men who have no one asking them the hard questions. Most men have no one who holds them accountable for how they are doing in the key areas of their lives. This comment from a businessman captures the dilemma:

> *It's interesting. Over the last several years I have become aware that I have no one to whom I must answer. As I have become more successful, everyone assumes I must*

> *have my act together. The worldly prestige that comes from success intimidates most people from asking how I am doing. There appears to be the presumption that since I am successful in business that every other area of my life is in order. Frankly, I operate without answering to anyone.*

Sound familiar? How do men fail? Some, of course, have spectacular failures where, in an instant of passion, they abruptly burst into flames, crash, and burn. But the most common way men get into trouble evolves from hundreds of tiny decisions—decisions which go undetected—that slowly, like water tapping on a rock, wear down a man's character. Not blatantly or precipitously, but subtly, over time, we get caught in a web of cutting corners and compromise, self-deceit and wrong thinking, which goes unchallenged by anyone in our lives.

What has God destined for every Christian according to Romans 8:29?

___

The ultimate purpose of accountability, then, is to help us become more like Jesus Christ in all our ways. Men who want to give themselves the best possible opportunity to succeed may want to consider establishing an accountable relationship. What do the following scriptures suggest about the value of accountability:

- Ecclesiastes 4:9-10

  ___

- Proverbs 27:6

  ___

- Proverbs 27:17

  ___

- Galatians 6:1-2

____

- Philippians 2:4

____

What is accountability, anyway? Here is a useful working definition of accountability for Christians:

> *To be regularly answerable for each of the key areas of our lives to qualified people.*

Let's explore the four aspects of the working definition and see how accountability works: *answerable, key areas, regularly,* and *qualified people.*

Answerable

In the work world everyone is accountable to someone—they must give an answer, whether to a boss, customers, or investors. What happens when people are not held accountable?

____

Unless we likewise are individually answerable on a regular basis for the key areas of our personal lives we, like sheep, will go astray. Yet, it is difficult to submit our lives to inspection by someone else.

What kind of answers should we give? The answers we give in an accountable relationship are primarily for the *goals* and the *standards* we should live by.

First, we should each set goals to help us accomplish our understanding of God's purpose and priorities for our lives. We need someone to whom we can be answerable—to give an accurate report—about how we are progressing toward those goals.

Second, the Bible delineates standards of character and conduct which apply to all Christians. We need people in our lives who challenge and encourage us to live up to those standards.

Do you now have, or ever had, anyone with whom you meet periodically to be accountable?

Key Areas

It is not the best foot we all put forward with which we need help. Rather, like the seven-eithths of an iceberg that is hidden below the surface, we need help in the areas of our lives often screened from view. Figure 1 shows how most of our conversation revolves around the cliché level of life—news, sports, and weather. But this is the tip of the iceberg—the visible you. The real you wrestles with gut-wrenching issues in the key areas of your life each day. We each need someone to help us navigate around the submerged dangers of an unexamined life.

Figure 1

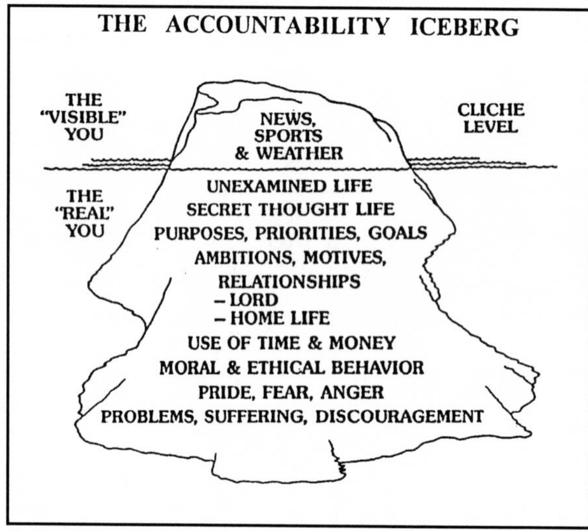

What are the key areas with which an accountable relationship should deal? Key areas in which we all need help include:

- Relationship With God
- Relationship With Wife

- Relationship With Children
- Use of Time and Money
- Moral and Ethical Behavior
- Areas of Personal Struggle (High Risk Areas)

Regularly

Regularly suggests the interval between contacts with accountability partners should be frequent and somewhat systematic. The best method is to meet weekly.

What do you talk about? The meetings should center on the key areas for accountability. *The Weekly One-Hour Accountability Check-Up* (Appendix A located at the end of this lesson) is a checklist of questions you could use to conduct a weekly meeting. You may find that some adaptation of this is helpful.

Qualified People

What does it mean to give an answer to qualified people? It would be of little value to have a man who has not yet had children to hold you accountable for how you are doing with the family. Consider the following ideas to find the best fit for your circumstances:

1. Pick someone who loves Christ, wants to see you succeed, and also wants to be held accountable.
2. Select someone who has skill and wisdom. A wise man has said, "Amateurs teach amateurs to be amateurs." What is the destiny of someone who is in an accountable relationship with someone wise according to Proverbs 13:20?
3. Consider having different men hold you accountable in different areas. Someone able to help with finances may not be able to help with an anger problem. (Of course, financial problems can cause emotional and relationship problems.)
4. Chances are high that an existing friend would be interested.
5. Women are out if you are a man. Too much temptation.
6. Wives are in, especially in areas of personal weakness where personal vulnerability is a sensitive issue.

7. Be sure to pick someone to help cover every area: moral, spiritual, financial and relational. It would be tragic to succeed in the family, but go bankrupt for inattention. Two out of three isn't good enough in accountability.
8. Pick a fellow struggler, not a boss.
9. Avoid asking men to help you who may have other agendas.
10. Pick someone who will be confidential. Let's face it. We've all been stung by betrayal. The price of an effective accountable relationship is personal vulnerability. In a friendship, personal vulnerability is *voluntary,* but in an accountable relationship it is *mandatory.* Personal vulnerability only comes when a trust relationship has been built. It takes time. It takes a willingness to risk. Neither rush it, nor be concerned that it takes a while. Eventually trust will come.

How to Get Started

Interested in teaming up with someone to help each other succeed? If so, you should give it a try. After praying for wisdom, select someone with whom you think you would be compatible. Explain that you are trying to build some accountability into your life. If they seem interested, have them review this material (which has been adapted from *The Man in the Mirror,* [Nashville: Thomas Nelson Publishers, 1989], Chapter 23).

Next, sit down together and plan a weekly meeting, pick the areas you want to cover, and start meeting. Discuss *The Weekly One-Hour Accountability Checkup* (attached). Keep it in a handy place—like your Bible.

Don't be fooled that it is easy. If it were, more men would be doing it. Accountability requires hard work, commitment, and lots of patience. The payoff, though, is worth the price.

Appendix A: The Weekly One-Hour Accountability Checkup

1. *Accountability:*

To be regularly answerable for each of the key areas of

our lives to qualified people.

2. *Questions to Start Off the Meeting:*
    a. How has God blessed you this week? (What went right?)
    b. What problem has consumed your thoughts this week? (What went wrong?)
3. *Spiritual Life:*
    a. Have you read God's Word daily? What has God been teaching/showing you?
    b. How long? Why not?
    c. Describe your prayers (for yourself, for others, praise, confession, gratitude). How is your relationship with Christ developing?
    d. How have you been tempted this week? How did you respond? Do you have any unconfessed sin in your life?
    e. Are you living in the Spirit?
    f. Did you worship in church this week? (Was your faith in Jesus strengthened? Was He honored?) Have you shared your faith? In what ways? How can you improve?
4. *Home Life:*
    a. How is it going with your wife (attitudes, time, intimacy, irritations, disappointments, her relationship with Christ)?
    b. How is it going with the kids (quantity and quality of time, values and beliefs, education, spiritual welfare)?
    c. How are your finances doing (debts, sharing, saving, stewardship)?
    d. How do you spend/invest your time around the house?
5. *Work Life:*

    How are things going on the job (career progress). How about relationships, temptations, work load, stress, problems, working too much?)
6. *Critical Concerns:*
    a. Do you feel in the center of God's will? Do you sense His peace? What are you wrestling with in your thought life?

   b. What have you done for someone else this week that can't be repaid (benevolence, encouragement, mercy, service to others)? Are your priorities in the right order?
   c. Is your moral and ethical behavior what it should be? How are you doing in your personal high-risk area?
   d. Is the visible you and the real you consistent in our relationship (if not, in what ways)?
7. *Prayer:*

   Close the one-hour accountability checkup with 10 to 15 minutes of prayer. Focus on concerns of the week.

Suggested Guidelines:

1. Try to ensure that each person gets equal air time: However, if one of you has a particularly hard struggle one week, be flexible enough to focus on that issue even if it takes the entire hour.
2. Let each person work through a section at a time, and then let the other(s) answer. This will keep things moving better.
3. Don't neglect the prayer time.
4. Try one-on-one. Small groups of three to five men can also work well if everyone speaks succinctly (one hour will go by very quickly).
5. Reread the chapter, "Accountability: The Missing Link," in Pat Morley's book, *The Man in the Mirror*, at least once every year and discuss the questions at the end of the chapter. You will be surprised how your understanding of accountability will change over the years.
6. Stick it out. You will want to quit, perhaps often. Ask God to strengthen you when you want to give up.
7. Hold each other accountable for the goals you each set for yourselves and to the standards of God's Word.
8. Never forget the purpose of accountability: To each day become more Christlike in all of your ways.

Remember it is Jesus who is the object of our search, our devotion, our sacrifice, and our affection. Anything less than intimacy with the living Lord will be a pallid achievement of your time together.

Finally, if you are uncomfortable with the format, feel free to alter these questions and type up your own accountability checklist. The substance is more important than the form. You may want to divide the key areas among more than one accountability partner.

A Final Reflection: Willpower

We need it to help shape our behavior. If we practice using willpower, over time we'll find that a particular behavior is weakened while our willpower is strengthened. Conversely, if we don't exercise willpower and instead indulge our sin, that behavior will become strengthened and willpower weakened.

Willpower is needed if we're to resist temptation and have victory over sin, but God is there to help us. The following suggestions may help you get back on the willpower path.

- Don't think sin will get better by itself. Sin never evolves into better behavior although a weakened conscience may obscure its evil deadliness.
- Don't neglect your spiritual basis. Although one particular sin may be frustrating, you can keep growing in other areas of your spiritual life. Your desire for victory over the sin combined with repentance, deepened prayer, Bible study, and more church involvement will add strength when you're ready to break loose from the besetting sin.
- Don't face temptation alone. Get an accountability partner whose willpower in your problem area is strong. You'll both benefit from the strong bond that will result from transparent sharing.
- Don't forget that God is in this with you. Believe that God can give you the needed willpower to face and conquer temptation. God's grace meets us when we decide to utilize His power.

Lesson 9: The Role of the Church

(Subject: Church)

> *Can I be a Christian without joining other Christians in a church? Yes, it is something like: being a soldier without an army, a seaman without a ship, a businessman without a business, a tuba player without an orchestra, a football player without a team or a bee without a hive* (Mrs. William P. Janzen).
>
> *The difference between listening to a radio sermon and going to church ... is almost like the difference between calling your girl on the phone and spending an evening with her* (Moody Monthly).
>
> *Though the church has many critics, it has no rivals* (Anonymous).

Memory Verse for This Lesson

> *Let us not give up meeting together, as some are in the habit of doing, but let us encourage one another—and all the more as you see the day approaching* (Hebrews 10:25).

What Is a Church?

Hurricane Katrina was the worst natural disaster in the history of the United States. Wind, tidal surge and the flooding in the New Orleans area due to levee and floodwall failure destroyed many churches of all denominations. Consider this question: When those buildings were blown down was the church destroyed?

To answer this question we must understand what actually constitutes a church. The word *church* (*ekklesia*) is conspicuously absent from all four gospels (except Matthew 16:18 and 18:17). Yet, it is interesting that Luke, one of the four gospel writers, uses the word 23 times in Acts. Surely then, the concept of church was something formulated by the early Christians in response to the death and resurrection of

Christ. All early Christian writers use *church* only for fellowships formed after the crucifixion and resurrection of Jesus. Why? Because it was the resurrection of Jesus and its announcement by His messengers that ushered in the church age. We live in the church age, which exists from the Resurrection until the second coming of Christ.

It is the apostle Paul who most shaped the concept of church. His starting point was always the proclamation of Christ crucified and resurrected. Paul emphasized that the coming together of believers was an essential element of church. Paul always understood the church as the "living, assembled congregation." Paul gave his instructions to particular local churches, but always kept in view that the church is "one." There is only one body of Christ, regardless of how many local and different manifestations there may be. And Christ is the head of the body. Christ is the groom and the church is His bride.

The church, then, is the body of believers worldwide. The church is also made up of individually organized groups of believers in local settings—the church universal and the church particular.

So is the church destroyed when the buildings are blown down? No. No in the sense that the church is not a place, but people—the body of believers. Yet, unless the believers have a place to assemble—to come together—they are disconnected from one another. So the place is important, but it could be a school building or a home church, as in many developing countries.

Moreover, the work of the church cannot be stopped by the destruction of its real estate. An illustration of this is as follows:

> *Stuart Rothberg is the senior pastor of Istrouma Baptist Church in Baton Rouge, Louisiana. Their church became a central shelter for hundreds of people as they fled from the aftermath of Hurricane Katrina during August of 2005. They retooled the way they operated their church and focused exclusively on meeting the needs of those who had sustained such enormous loss. While speaking*

of their experience in caring for these evacuees, Rothberg cited a study conducted by Louisiana State University in the months following that catastrophic storm. They surveyed people displaced by the hurricane and asked which agency responded best to the disaster. The number one answer was "the church." We can certainly be grateful for groups like FEMA and the Red Cross, but there is nothing to compare with the church (Stuff I Learned From The Storm, Stuart Rothberg, Sagemont Church, January 4, 2006).

Why Do We Need a Church?

Is Christianity at its core essentially a personal experience or a group experience? As someone has said, "God doesn't have any grandchildren." Each person must stand individually before God. We each become a follower of Jesus individually through faith and repentance. In this sense Christianity is a personal experience. Salvation is personal. On the other hand, the church is the place where we work out the lordship of Christ in our lives. We become a Christian individually, but we follow Him in a group. As John Wesley put it: "The Bible knows nothing of solitary religion."

Those who struggle with making their *Savior* their *Lord* are often the same ones who don't sense the need to be connected to a vital local church of fellow believers. Our culture is particularly narcissistic and self-centered. People often don't make a commitment to a local church because they are more into getting than giving. They want to get a blessing, not be one. The Bible calls for a radically different kind of relationship to other believers.

The first Biblical example of church is found in Acts 2:42-47. List at least five characteristics of this early church:

1. ______________________________

2. ______________________________

3. ______________________________________

4. ______________________________________

5. ______________________________________

There are at least five major purposes for attending church.

1. Worship: Experience With God

The overarching purpose of church is to worship the living God. The Bible exhorts and commands us to worship God. To worship literally means to lie prostrate, to fall facedown, to stoop down, to render religious homage. It is to show proper reverence, respect, awe, and holy fear. It is to express your love for God in a tangible way.

Why do we need to worship God? First, because He is worthy to receive our worship. Second, because He longs to meet with us. Third, because worship brings us into the presence of our holy God.

Worship is meant to be a lifestyle. The attitude of the inner man is what's important, rather than a place. The cross of Jesus Christ is the central focal point of our worship. Worship can be personal or corporate. Corporate worship is what we call church.

What are the ways we can worship God and the Lord Jesus Christ? We worship God by becoming quiet before Him, by entering into His presence with a worshipful attitude. The 16th-century Reformers believed that to have church required the preaching of God's Word and the administration of the sacraments—baptism and Communion. Certainly these are part of worshiping God. Also included in worship are prayer, singing, praising, and thanksgiving.

2. Fellowship: Encouragement From God

In Acts 2:42, to what did the believers devote themselves?

____

The mutual need for fellowship with other believers constitutes a major purpose for attending church. "All the believers were together and had everything in common.... Every day they continued to meet together in the temple courts. They broke bread in their homes and ate together with glad and sincere hearts" (Acts 2:44,46).

Koinonia, the Greek word for fellowship, refers to a partnership. It literally means participation or social intercourse, and translates as communion, communication, and fellowship. It is always used in a spiritual sense, never in a secular sense.

Believers need each other for spiritual, prayer, emotional, and social support. The new command Christ gave is to love each other as He loved us. We cannot love people whom we don't know. We cannot love people unless we are connected to them in some way. The church gives us a larger family of which we can be a part.

Perhaps the greatest value of fellowship is *encouragement.* Life in the world is filled with struggles. It is good to have a community of caring people with whom to share not only our joys, but our sorrows. "Courage," according to Webster, is "the state of mind or spirit that enables one to face hardship or disaster with confidence and resolution." What, then, is encouragement? To "encourage someone is to *inspire* them to have courage—to face their hardships with confidence and resolution."

3. Growth: Knowledge of God

The Lord's last earthly words have been appropriately named the Great Commission. He told His followers to "go and make disciples of all nations, baptizing them ... and teaching them to obey everything I have commanded you" (Matthew 28:19, 20).

The church is a place to learn about God. The preaching and teaching of God's Word—what it *says,* its *meaning,* its *message,* and how it *applies* are critical elements in the life of a vibrant church. Growth in the *knowledge* of God is just as important as growth in *love* for God.

4. Service: Work for God

What is the message of Ephesians 2:10?

___

Every Christian is called to serve Christ through personal ministry, or service.

According to Ephesians 4:11, 12, what is the role of the church in your personal ministry or service?

___

The church is the principal outlet for discerning your spiritual gifts, becoming equipped to serve, and finding an outlet to serve as part of the body of Christ and to the broken, hurting world.

Consider for a moment what America would look like without the church. Where would the great hospitals, schools, and universities be? Where would the feeding stations and the rescue missions be? Would anyone be doing inner-city youth work or providing homes for unwed mothers? Where would be the voices calling out for abstinence from premarital sex or for the right to life be? Who would be the voice of justice, and the hands of mercy? Who would be the feet of the gospel of salvation? Who would be the light in the darkness, the salt seeking to preserve society and culture?

What would America look like without the church? We need only look to Western Europe to see the answer to that. The secularization of the society has led to a continent without hope, which in turn has led to a free fall in their birth rate. People who have no hope in eternity have no reason to send children into the future. This is why the rise of Islam within Europe is so dangerous. The followers of Allah will fill what the followers of secularism will abandon.

5. Accountability: Walk With God

What do Romans 14:12 and Matthew 12:36 say about accountability?

Howard Ball says, "The Christian life is not difficult. It's impossible." No Christian ever led a vibrant, obedient life on his own. Without the help of a few friends to keep us on track we, too, like sheep will go astray.

Chuck Colson says this: "Fellowship is more than unconditional love that wraps its arms around someone who is hurting. It is also tough love that holds one fast to the truth.... For most Christians, the support side of the equation comes more easily than accountability and the subsequent discipline involved" (Charles Colson, *The Body*. Dallas: Word Publishing, 1992, p. 130).

A major purpose of the church is to provide a framework for accountability. Every Biblical church has some form of church discipline. Beyond that, the most successful churches link people together in smaller groups where there is increased visibility. Visibility creates accountability.

We become Christians in a single, dazzling moment of surrender, but then we must work out that salvation through the peaks and valleys of life in this world. Such a feat is best accomplished with the help of some like-minded people who will help keep you on track. If Christ is your Savior, have you made Him your Lord? Church is the place where we work out the details of the lordship of Christ over us.

These are five main purposes for attending church. Which of these purposes are being fulfilled in your life? Which are not?

1. Worship: Yes ______ No _________
2. Fellowship: Yes ______ No _________
3. Personal Growth: Yes ______ No _________
4. Service: Yes ______ No _________
5. Accountability: Yes ______ No _________

What Makes a Good Church?

Anyone who simply looks through the Yellow Pages or searches on the Internet will quickly realize that there are many kinds of churches. But, to borrow an expression from Abraham Lincoln, all churches are not created equal. So how do we know what makes a good church?

There are two essentials for a good church: proper beliefs and proper worship.

1. Beliefs

A church is ultimately defined by what it knows to be true, not what it thinks feels good. Because of the large number of denominations in existence, many are afraid to even discuss beliefs (usually termed *doctrine.*) However, as the great Bible teacher J. Vernon McGee used to say, "Those that won't stand for something will fall for anything."

To illustrate the essential beliefs of a good church, we will use the doctrinal statements of two very different churches: the "Declaration of Faith" of the Church of God, the statement of a modern Pentecostal church, and the "Thirty-Nine Articles" of the Church of England, a Reformation-era (1500s) statement. Although at first glance it looks to be an "apples and oranges" business, the two are historically tied through the Wesleyan Movement. The ties that bind believers and churches are stronger than the divisions that separate them.

With this in mind, let's look at some core beliefs that define a true Christian church:

- God the Creator exists in three persons, Father, Son, and Holy Spirit.
  - ⊙ We believe in one God eternally existing in three persons; namely, the Father, Son, and Holy Ghost (Declaration 2).
  - ⊙ THERE is but one living and true God, everlasting, without body, parts, or passions; of infinite power, wisdom, and goodness; the maker and preserver of all things both visible and invisible. And in unity of this Godhead there be three Persons, of one substance, power, and eternity; the Father,

the Son, and the Holy Ghost (Article I).

- Jesus, God's Son and God himself, born of a virgin, was crucified and rose from the dead to sit at the right hand of the Father.
  - ⊙ We believe that Jesus Christ is the only begotten Son of the Father, conceived of the Holy Ghost, and born of the Virgin Mary. That Jesus was crucified, buried, and raised from the dead. That He ascended to heaven and is today at the right hand of the Father as the Intercessor (Declaration 3).
  - ⊙ THE Son, which is the Word of the Father, begotten from everlasting of the Father, the very and eternal God, and of one substance with the Father, took man's nature in the womb of the blessed Virgin, of her substance: so that two whole and perfect natures, that is to say, the Godhead and manhood, were joined together in one person, never to be divided, whereof is one Christ, very God and very man, who truly suffered, was crucified, dead, and buried, to reconcile His Father to us, and to be a sacrifice, not only for original guilt, but also for all actual sins of men (Article II).
- Men are lost sinners, only reconciled to God through repentance and faith in Jesus Christ as the propitiation for their sins.
  - ⊙ We believe that all have sinned and come short of the glory of God and that repentance is commanded of God for all and necessary for forgiveness of sins; that justification, regeneration, and the new birth are wrought by faith in the blood of Jesus Christ (Declarations 4 and 5).
  - ⊙ ORIGINAL sin ... is the fault and corruption of the nature of every man ... whereby man is very far gone from original righteousness, and ... deserveth God's wrath and damnation. ... WE are accounted righteous before God, only for the merit of our Lord and Saviour Jesus Christ by faith, and not for our own works or deservings. Wherefore that we are justified by faith only is a most wholesome doctrine, and very full of comfort... (Articles IX, XI).
- The Bible is the authoritative, inerrant Word of God.
  - ⊙ We believe in the verbal inspiration of the Bible (Declaration 1).
  - ⊙ HOLY Scriptures containeth all things necessary to salvation:

so that whatsoever is not read therein, nor may be proved thereby, is not to be required of any man, that it should be believed as an article of the faith, or be thought requisite or necessary to salvation ... (Article VI).

- Christ established sacraments (or ordinances) for the church to practice. Following the Reformation, most non-Catholic or non-Eastern Orthodox churches practice baptism and the Lord's Supper, while some, following John 13, include footwashing.
  - ⊙ We believe in water baptism by immersion, and all who repent should be baptized in the name of the Father, and of the Son, and of the Holy Ghost... In the Lord's Supper and washing of the saints' feet (Declarations 10 and 12).
  - ⊙ SACRAMENTS ordained of Christ be not only badges or tokens of Christian men's profession, but rather they be certain sure witnesses and effectual signs of grace and God's good will towards us, by the which He doth work invisibly in us, and doth not only quicken, but also strengthen and confirm, our faith in Him. There are two Sacraments ordained of Christ our Lord in the Gospel, that is to say, Baptism and the Supper of the Lord... (Article XXV).
- Jesus Christ will return to judge the earth and establish His kingdom; all will be resurrected, the just to eternal life and the lost to eternal death.
  - ⊙ We believe in the premillennial second coming of Jesus. First, to resurrect the righteous dead and to catch away the living saints to Him in the air. Second, to reign on the earth a thousand years; in the bodily resurrection; eternal life for the righteous, and eternal punishment for the wicked (Declarations 13 and 14).
  - ⊙ I believe ... in Jesus Christ ... Who ... sitteth on the right hand of God the Father Almighty: From thence he shall come to judge the quick and the dead ...The Resurrection of the body, And the Life everlasting (Apostles' Creed, included through Article VIII).

Discuss each of these points. Why are they important? Can any be left out for a Christian church? Why or why not?

2. Worship Style

Churches vary widely in the style of worship, even within one denomination or tradition. So how do we know what worship style is correct?

Write down John 4:24.

Christian worship must be both in spirit and in truth. It must be led by God and must draw people towards God. Although it's important to people, worship style is secondary to its goals. Different styles exist to connect with different types of people and lead them to their heavenly Father.

Gordon MacDonald has identified what he calls *leading instincts of the soul.* His thesis is that different people are led into the worship of God along six different lines. Different people best communicate with God in different ways. MacDonald identifies six instincts.[1]

1. *Majesty: The Aesthetic Instinct.* The aesthetic seeks to be overwhelmed by the majesty of God. He is happiest when the worship environment includes beauty, order, tradition, and artistic integrity. He is a traditionalist who may not appreciate overly sentimental worship or songs and prayer that seems presumptuously familiar. One of the best-known examples of this is Eastern Orthodox worship. A thousand years ago, when Prince Vladimir of Kiev sent a delegation to the Greek Orthodoxy center in Constantinople to find out what kind of religion he wanted for his realm, the Ukrainians were so overwhelmed by the experience that they did not know

whether they were in heaven or on earth.

2. *Joy: The Experiential Instinct.* The experientialist wants to *feel* the presence of God and respond with a full range of emotions, including clapping, singing, prayer, weeping, laughing, and more. This instinct seems to bind people of diverse races and cultures most powerfully. This kind of worship is commonly found in Pentecostal churches, which in part explains why these churches are readily cross-cultural.
3. *Achievement: The Activist Instinct.* The activist sees everything through the lens of service. The world needs to be changed, and he wants to be part of it. Whether by helping the poor, spreading the gospel, or changing the system, the activist is energized by doing Kingdom work. He feels closest to God when he is making a contribution. Such a worship style is summed up by the motto of the Benedictine order of monks: "To work is to pray."
4. *Listening: The Contemplative Instinct.* The contemplative is profoundly concerned about the inner life, about opening up to God in the quiet of his own soul. He is impressed by the mystery of God, and wants to sense His presence. This can only be gained when he shuns the din of the day and presses himself to be still. The "pre-Vatican II" Roman Catholic church was very strong on this kind of worship.
5. *Truth: The Student Instinct.* The student loves truth. The study of the Bible forms the core of his worship style. He is happiest at a church that emphasizes the preaching and teaching of the Word. He is a little suspicious of those who sense God's presence or sense God speaking to them. He is more objective. Churches in the Reformed tradition (Presbyterian, etc.) generally worship in this way.
6. *Love: The Relational Instinct.* The relationalist finds God most present when people are bonded together in fellowship, worship, or mutual support. He is torn when there is conflict, lifted high when the walls come tumbling down. He feels closest to God when the brothers and sisters are in harmony. Small groups are natural settings for this kind of worship.

MacDonald suggests that we each have a natural inclination toward two or three and a curiosity toward one or two more. Jesus possessed all six, and in perfect balance. He left His throne in heaven and became one of us so that we could be with Him in eternity. Jesus met us on our level in becoming man, and continues to do so in the varying styles of worship. Our worship is also a preparation of the day when we will worship Him directly in front of His throne for eternity.

A Final Reflection

A man called the pastor to say he wanted to join the church. But he said he didn't want to attend every week, he wasn't interested in reading the Bible or prayer, outreach wasn't one of his interests, he didn't want to be a teacher or a leader, and he absolutely was not going to give 10 percent of his money to the church.

The pastor commended him for his interest in joining the church, but suggested that the church he would really enjoy was located across town. The man took directions and hung up. When he found the church, it was an abandoned church building, boarded up and ready for demolition.

Appendix: Church of God Declaration of Faith

We Believe:

- In the verbal inspiration of the Bible.
- In one God eternally existing in three persons; namely, the Father, Son, and Holy Ghost.
- That Jesus Christ is the only begotten Son of the Father, conceived of the Holy Ghost, and born of the Virgin Mary. That Jesus was crucified, buried, and raised from the dead. That He ascended to heaven and is today at the right hand of the Father as the Intercessor.
- That all have sinned and come short of the glory of God and that repentance is commanded of God for all and necessary for forgiveness of sins.

- That justification, regeneration, and the new birth are wrought by faith in the blood of Jesus Christ.
- In sanctification subsequent to the new birth, through faith in the blood of Christ; through the Word, and by the Holy Ghost.
- Holiness to be God's standard of living for His people.
- In the baptism with the Holy Ghost subsequent to a clean heart.
- In speaking with other tongues as the Spirit gives utterance and that it is the initial evidence of the baptism in the Holy Ghost.
- In water baptism by immersion, and all who repent should be baptized in the name of the Father, and of the Son, and of the Holy Ghost.
- Divine healing is provided for all in the atonement.
- In the Lord's Supper and washing of the saints' feet.
- In the premillennial second coming of Jesus. First, to resurrect the righteous dead and to catch away the living saints to Him in the air. Second, to reign on the earth a thousand years.
- In the bodily resurrection; eternal life for the righteous, and eternal punishment for the wicked.

---

[1] Gordon MacDonald, *Discipleship Journal,* July/August 1992, pp. 32, 33.

Lesson 10: How to Witness Effectively

(Subject: Witnessing)

You are a Christian today because somebody cared. Now it's your turn (Warren Wiersbe).

Kindness has converted more sinners than zeal, eloquence, or learning (Henrietta Mears).

It is the Holy Spirit, not we, who converts an individual .... Let us never naively think that we have converted a soul and brought him to Jesus Christ.... No one calls Jesus Lord except by the Holy Spirit (Paul Little).

Memory Verse for This Lesson

But you will receive power when the Holy Spirit comes on you; and you will be my witnesses in Jerusalem, and in all Judea and Samaria, and to the ends of the earth (Acts 1:8).

The Case for Witnessing: A Testimony by Pat Morley

My brother Robert returned from Vietnam psychologically damaged. When a Billy Graham film came to town I invited Robert to attend.

After the movie I asked Robert if he had ever given his life to Christ. He answered no. Then I asked him if he would like to. He said yes. Using Campus Crusade for Christ's "The Four Spiritual Laws," which outlines the basics of the gospel, I had the privilege and joy of helping my brother place his faith in Jesus Christ for the forgiveness of his sins and eternal life.

But Robert was still psychologically damaged. He decided to move to Brownsville, Texas, to become a commercial fisherman. One summer Robert and I saw each other at a family retreat. I asked my brother, "How is it going on your spiritual pilgrimage?"

His countenance became serious and Robert replied, "Well, I want you to know I still believe, but you need to know it's really hard for me."

Three months later I received a call. It was not a call I expected, but not one that surprised me either. It seems my brother had been out at sea for a couple of weeks. Upon arriving at port, his comrades invited him to join them at a tavern for some beers, to which he agreed.

After sitting at a bar for two hours, Robert passed out, fell on the floor, and started turning blue. Some of his mates picked him up by his arms and legs and carried him like some frumpy oversized, stuffed rag doll into the back room of the little pub. Then, even though he was turning blue, they laid him on the cold stone floor, turned around, and walked away. Robert never regained consciousness.

Why should you be a witness? Because you just never know what is going to happen in life—or when.

We must come to grips with where Jesus wants us to center our lives. What is the pivotal point of His teaching? On what key point does the teaching of Jesus turn? What is the central issue that concerns Him? What overarching idea epitomized His life?

Why Jesus Came

Jesus came "to seek and to save what was lost" (Luke 19:10). "Here is a trustworthy saying that deserves full acceptance: Christ Jesus came into the world to save sinners" (1 Timothy 1:15). Jesus healed the sick, cast out demons, raised the dead, and performed one-of-a-kind miracles. But were these the highest point—the ultimate end—of His life and ministry? No, these were primarily the means to another end. To what end did Jesus perform these mind-boggling feats? And why is the body of Christ empowered to do "even greater things than these?" (John 14:12). Peter explained it on the first Day of Pentecost, "Jesus of Nazareth was a man *accredited* by God to you by miracles, wonders and signs" (Acts 2:22). Like a school or university's education is validated in the marketplace by accreditation, the signs and wonders of Jesus Christ—and those who still do them in His name—are to bear witness to the *purpose* and *authority* of Jesus Christ.

Everything Jesus did contributed to His purpose. No step Jesus ever took or word He ever uttered was meant for any purpose except to point men toward the knowledge of the kingdom of God. Jesus came with the authority to offer forgiveness of sins and salvation to all who believe.

The Command to Witness

Evangelism is not a matter of mere human sympathy. Christianity is not a matter of dramatic human helps to ease the burden of daily living. That would be a good idea, but not a God idea. Instead, evangelism is a command based upon the authority of Jesus Christ to baptize and disciple sinners into everlasting life. "All authority in heaven and on earth has been given to me. Therefore go and make disciples ... " (Matthew 28:18, 19). Evangelism is the God idea that summarizes the Bible: Redemption for sinners who repent and believe.

Witnessing is a *command*, not a *suggestion*. One day a man said, "I don't share my faith because I don't have the gift of evangelism." Some people do receive a special gift of evangelism (see Ephesians 4:11). Some, then, will use their gift of evangelism to lead people to the feet of the Master. It may even come easy to them. They are the sales department. But every other department ultimately supports sales, for if nothing is sold then there is no need for service and support.

Those among us who do not have the *gift* of evangelism will have to rely on our willingness to obey Jesus' *command* to bear witness. We will work in children's ministries, reach out to the poor, teach and train new and mature believers, care for people in crisis, show mercy and do works of service. And yet, unless our service includes sensitivity to how we may win the lost we labor in vain, for the ultimate purpose of God is to save lost sinners, not merely bandage humanity's mortal wounds.

All of our good deeds, good works, and Christian service should be focused by and filtered through Christ's command to be witnesses to the life-changing power of faith in Jesus. Paul wrote words to his young protégé Timothy we should all apply, "Do the work of an evangelist, discharge all the duties of your ministry" (2 Timothy 4:5). Evangelism is where Jesus centered His life. By His authority, it is where He wants us to center ours.

What does Proverbs 11:30 tell us?

____

Consider these four reasons we should witness and answer the questions:

1. Christ Commands Every Christian to Be a Witness

Read Matthew 28:18-20 and answer these questions:

- How much authority does Jesus have?

  ____

- What does He command us to do?

  ____

Notice that Jesus doesn't say, "Therefore, 37 percent of you go and make disciples ..." He commands all of us to go.

2. Witnessing Leads People to Christ, Which Is How People Inherit Eternal Life

What does Acts 4:12 say?

____

According to John 14:6, how many ways can people come to the Father?

____

3. Without Christ Men and Women Are Eternally Lost

Who did Jesus come to seek and save? (Luke 19:10).

____

What percentage of people have sinned? (Romans 3:23).

____

What is the wage of sin? (Romans 6:23).

____

Does God send people to eternal punishment? (Matthew 25:46).

____

A survey at an Urbana Conference, a gathering of America's most missions-minded youth, revealed that only 37 percent believed that the lost are *really* lost. People often believe God will surely provide another way; that a loving God would not send people to hell. Yet, the Bible clearly tells us that the only way to salvation is through Jesus Christ, and those who are not so saved are sent away to eternal punishment. This is a serious matter that deserves full consideration. It is a significant motivator to witness.

4. God Has Given Us Power to Witness

This is a good time to review the appendix of Chapter 4, "Power to Witness for Christ." Reading Acts 1:8, where does the power to witness come from?

Many times, we think that we are solely responsible both for the technique and the results of personal evangelism. But God has empowered us to witness.

Write down John 12:32.

Now that Jesus has been both crucified and raised from the dead, who will draw people to God? Witnessing power encompasses both those of us who witness and those to whom we are witnessing.

Evangelistic Witnessing

There is a profound difference between witnessing and evangelistic witnessing. Unless witnessing is oriented to bring people to the decision to receive Jesus, it merely improves our reputation.

While in high school and before he knew Christ, Dr. James Kennedy greatly admired a young man in his school. Only after becoming a Christian did he discover the young man was Christian. He never shared his faith, so the focus was on his fine personality, not Christ.

Oswald Chambers, in *My Utmost for His Highest,* cautions us this way:

> *What a wonderful personality! What a fascinating man! Such a marvelous insight! What chance has the Gospel of God through all that? ... If a man attracts by his personality, then the appeal is along that line; if he is identified with his Lord's personality, then the appeal is along the line of what Jesus Christ can do.*

We must be careful that we do not merely tell people what Christ has done for us, but how they too, can know Him. To merely tell them what He has done for us is to tell them how we found great treasure, but hide from them how they can find some, too.

Why is witnessing without sharing Christ useless?

The Two Parts to Effective Witnessing

Effective witnessing usually includes both a *testimony* and a presentation of the *gospel.* A testimony is telling someone what God has done for you; a gospel presentation is telling someone what God can do for them.

A testimony relates your own personal experience with Christ. It builds rapport. People will often relate to your own search for authentic meaning and significance. A personal testimony makes the gospel relevant to the person with whom you are sharing. At the end of this lesson is a Three-Minute Testimony Worksheet. Complete this before your discipleship appointment and be prepared to present it aloud to your discipler.

A testimony, however, without a presentation of the gospel is akin to telling someone terminally ill with cancer about a miracle drug that cured your cancer, but neglecting to tell them how they can get it, too. Once you have given your personal testimony, be sure to explain the gospel to them.

Methods of Sharing Your Faith

When you discover a method of witnessing that works for you hold fast to it. Some frown on passing out tracts on street corners as too impersonal. Others scowl at lifestyle evangelism that befriends people over the long term as too slow. But *the best method of witnessing is the one you will use.*

No one method or style of evangelism is more valid than another. Francis Schaeffer commented on the need for flexibility in method. He wrote:

> *Each generation of the church in each setting has*

> *the responsibility of communicating the gospel in understandable terms, considering the language and thought-forms of that setting.*

The essential issues in evangelism are: Is it faithful to the truth? Is it honoring to God? Does it depend upon the Holy Spirit to produce fruit? Does it produce fruit? Any method that honors Christ and produces fruit is valid. Here are some examples:

— Inviting neighbors to your evangelistic church services

— Inviting associates to an evangelistic Bible study

— Taking training to learn how to share your faith

— Calling on church visitors

— Passing out tracts door-to-door

— Taking a friend to lunch to explain the gospel

— Giving Bibles to nonbelievers in hospitals

— Inviting associates to community outreach events

— Organizing an evangelistic prayer breakfast, luncheon, or dinner party with an outside speaker[1]

— Giving money to evangelistic ministries

— Setting up chairs for a missions banquet

— Raising money for an evangelistic ministry or minister

— Working in a drug, alcohol, or pregnancy program that points people to Christ

— Jail ministries

— Ministry to the poor that is gospel centered.

Put a number next to each of the methods above based on the following scale:

1. I regularly do this now.
2. I would like to begin doing this.
3. I could do this if I received some training.
4. I could never do this.

Are you doing enough? What practical steps can you take to be a more effective witness?

God made each of us different. We need to respect, even treasure, these differences. The Holy Spirit has anointed countless different methods to be the means of spreading the gospel. Still, though the message can be communicated through many methods, we can ill afford to ever forget that it is a single message: belief in Jesus Christ. It is why He came.

Three-Minute Testimony Worksheet

Complete the following three-point outline with the personal story of your relationship with Christ. It is extremely important to write out your testimony. As Francis Bacon said, "Writing makes an exact man." Commit it to memory. *Once you have memorized your three-minute testimony you will enter into a new zone of confidence in witnessing.* No one can ever take this work away from you.

1. *Before You Gave Your Life to Christ.* Remembering your audience, what were the problems you faced? What were you looking for in life? What did you do to find meaning, purpose, significance, and peace of mind?

   ---

2. *When You Trusted Christ With Your Life.* When and how did you first hear the gospel? How did you react? What caused you to hesitate? Why did you decide to receive Christ?

3. *Since You Have Given Your Life to Christ.* What are some specific changes that have occurred? Were the changes sudden or gradual? What does Jesus Christ mean to you personally?

Tips:

- Start with an attention-getting sentence.
- Avoid denominations.
- Be positive.
- Avoid religious lingo.
- Tell stories.
- Close with a punch line.

PRESENTING THE GOSPEL

Once you have given your testimony, you can proceed to present the gospel. Develop a conversational style by asking introductory questions.

1. What is your concept of God?
    - Notice that this is an open-ended question—they cannot give just a yes or no answer.
    - You will find out if the person views God as a harsh judgmental God or just a Santa Claus type God.
2. How would you describe your *relationship* with God?
    - This approach lets the people who are unsaved talk about their spiritual beliefs.
    - Learn to listen. Listening has been referred to as unspoken flattery. Reply in a way that allows people the freedom to talk. This does not mean we should agree with them, it is merely showing them the respect that all people want.
3. At what point are you in your *spiritual* beliefs or pursuits?
    - Again be sure to listen to them. God gave us two ears and only one mouth, and we should use them proportionately! We probably need to listen twice as much as we talk.
4. If you were God, what *requirements* would you make for people to get into heaven?
    - If you can get them to answer this question, you will discover what they think they need to do to get into heaven.
    - How they answer this question will give an indication of the depth (or lack) of their understanding of the concept of God and the work of Jesus on the cross.

Once you have done this, you can proceed with the same four-point gospel presentation you were presented with in Lesson 1.

A FINAL REFLECTION: ANYONE CAN TALK; FEW CAN FISH

Now it came to pass that a group existed who called themselves fishermen.

And, lo, there were many fish in the waters, all around. In fact, the whole area was surrounded by streams and lakes filled with fish, and the fish were hungry.

Week after week, month after month, and year after year, those who called themselves fishermen met and talked about their call to go fishing.

Continually they searched for new and better methods of fishing and for new and better definitions of fishing. They sponsored costly nationwide and worldwide congresses to discuss fishing and hear about all the ways of fishing, such as the new fishing equipment, or whether any new bait was discovered.

These fishermen built large and beautiful buildings called Fishing Headquarters. The plea was that everyone should be a fisherman and every fisherman should fish.

One thing they didn't do; however, was fish. All of the fishermen seemed to agree that what was needed was a board that could challenge fishermen to be faithful in fishing.

The board was formed by those who had the great vision and courage to speak about fishing, to define fishing, and to promote the idea of fishing in faraway streams and lakes where many other fish of different colors lived. Large, elaborate and expensive training centers were built whose purpose was to teach fishermen how to fish. Those who taught had doctorates in fishology.

But the teachers did not fish; they only taught fishing. Some spent much time in study and travel to learn the history of fishing and to see faraway places where the founding fathers did great fishing in centuries past. They lauded the faithful fishermen of years earlier who handed down the idea of fishing.

Many who felt the call to be fishermen responded. They were commissioned and sent to fish. And they went off to foreign lands ...to teach fishing.

Now it's true that many of the fishermen sacrificed and put up with all kinds of difficulties. Some lived near the water and bore the smell of dead fish every day. They received the ridicule of some who made fun of their fisherman clubs. They anguished over those who were not committed enough to attend the weekly meetings to talk about fishing.

After all, were they not following the one who said, "Follow me and I will make you fishers of men"?

Imagine how hurt some were when one day a person suggested that those who didn't catch fish were really not fishermen, no matter how much they claimed to be. Yet it did sound correct.

Is a person a fisherman if year after year he never catches a fish? Is one following if he isn't fishing?

If Christ were to return to this earth today in physical form, would He find us fishing, or would He find us organizing, talking about fishing, and making plans to build the best Fishing Headquarters anywhere? (Source unknown).

---

[1] An excellent example of this is the Resurrection Breakfast program, available from Men's Discipleship International.

Lesson 11: How to Determine Your Spiritual Gifts

(Subject: Spiritual Gifts)

> *A gift is a Spirit-given ability for Christian service* (Leslie B. Flynn).
>
> *A spiritual gift is a special spiritual ability given by the Holy Spirit to every believer to be used in serving others through a personal ministry* (Leslie B. Flynn).
>
> *Practice of the Biblical doctrine of gifts untaps reservoirs of godly manpower, thaws out frozen assets, roots out unemployment among saints, reflects the universal priesthood of believers, and edifies the church* (Leslie B. Flynn).

Memory Verse for This Lesson

> *Each one should use whatever gift he has received to serve others, faithfully administering God's grace in its various forms* (1 Peter 4:10).

Introduction

God is building a family of people who will love Him, care for one another, and reach out to others. This family is called the church, or the body of Christ.

The central purpose of Jesus Christ coming to earth and being human—which is called the incarnation, or coming into human flesh—was to meet us where we are and bring us to where He is. The church, under the direction and empowerment of the Holy Spirit, has the task of continuing that work of meeting human need—of being Christ's hands, feet, etc., until His bodily return.

Take a look at 1 Corinthians 12:14-26. Why is it important for the human body to have all of its parts to function?

____

What is this passage saying about the body of Christ? Is it the same or different?

____

As in any family or business, if everyone in the church did the same job then important functions would be left undone. If everyone wanted to manage the business, who would do the selling? the purchasing? the manufacturing? the bookkeeping? If everyone wanted to teach, who would visit the sick? take care of the facilities? win the lost? remember the poor?

Like any other institution, the church works best when a division of labor puts different people to work in different roles. In the church God has ordained to give special spiritual abilities to permit the smooth functioning of the Body. These special abilities are called *spiritual gifts.*

No man will find himself in useful service for the kingdom of Christ until he discovers how God has uniquely blessed him with spiritual gifts, and what those spiritual gifts are.

About Spiritual Gifts

To whom is spiritual gifts given? Every believer receives at least one spiritual gift. "Now *to each one* the manifestation of the Spirit is given for the common good" (1 Corinthians 12:7, emphasis added).

Who gives these spiritual gifts? The Holy Spirit determines our spiritual gifts. "He gives them to each one, just as he determines" (1 Corinthians 12:11). "Each man has his own gift from God" (1 Corinthians 7:7).

How should we use our spiritual gifts? The purpose of our spiritual gifts is to serve Christ by serving others, helping to fulfill the Great Commission. "Each one should use whatever gift he has received *to serve others*.... "Our responsibility is to be faithful." "... to serve others, *faithfully* administering God's grace in its various forms" (1 Peter 4:10, emphasis added).

1. According to 1 Corinthians 12:1, what is the purpose of the 12th chapter?

   ____

2. Read 1 Corinthians 12:7. Who is given spiritual gifts?

   ____

   Why are they given?

   ____

3. From 1 Corinthians 12:11, how does the Holy Spirit determine how gifts are given?

   ____

4. What does 1 Corinthians 12:12 suggest about the value of diverse spiritual gifts?

   ____

5. Read 1 Corinthians 12:14-20. In verse 18, how has God arranged people in the Body?

   ____

   What point does this passage make?

   ____

6. Read Romans 12:3-8. To whom does each member of the Body belong according to Romans 12:5?

   ____

7. Ephesians 4:11-13 lists a number of spiritual gifts. According to verse 12, why were these spiritual gifts given?

   ____

8. Read 1 Peter 4:9-11. According to verse 10, how should each one of us use whatever gift(s) we have received?

   ____

According to verse 11, what is the ultimate purpose of faithfully using our spiritual gifts?

Understanding Different Gifts

The first step to find your niche in effective service in the body of Christ is to understand your spiritual gifts. It would be foolish to try to become a salesman if you prefer to work with numbers. In the same way we pursue vocational employment based upon our aptitudes and abilities, we pursue our spiritual service based on an understanding of how God has uniquely gifted us.

There are basically two types of gifts: manifestation gifts and ministry gifts.

1. Manifestation Gifts

These are also known as the *sign* gifts. These gifts are temporary and are not related to natural abilities. Because of this, they are not directly connected to the individual's position in the church; they are the immediate move of the Holy Spirit.

They are listed in 1 Corinthians 12:8-10. There are nine of them:

1. *Word of wisdom.* A specific utterance giving God's wisdom for a particular time and situation.
2. *Word of knowledge.* Speaking a divine revelation of an event or fact that is not known by the speaker.
3. *Faith.* Not normal saving faith but a special gift of faith to give confidence for a particular situation or task.
4. *Healing.* A special gift of God for healing to self and others. As was the case with Jesus' own ministry, the main purpose of divine healing is to show God's power to those who are lost.
5. *Miracles.* Similar in concept to healing except that it involves nonmedical situations which need God's power.
6. *Prophecy.* Speaking what's on God's mind for the present and future.
7. *Discerning of spirits.* Gives a person the ability to know the

nature of the spirits around them.

8. *Tongues.* Not the speaking in tongues we discussed in Lesson 4, but special messages given in an unknown tongue.
9. *Interpretation of tongues.* The companion gift of tongues, to interpret the message in the language of the people. These last two gifts usually are manifested when Christians are gathered together (church service, small group, etc.).

It needs to be emphasized that, with these gifts especially, the emphasis is on the gift, not the one manifesting the gift.

Write down 2 Corinthians 4:7.

____

____

What does this teach us about where everything that we receive from God—including spiritual gifts—comes from? Can we take the credit? How do we compare with what God has given us?

____

____

2. Ministry Gifts

A frequent discussion point with spiritual gifts is the question, "Do spiritual gifts have any relation to our human abilities?" It's not an either/or answer but a both/and answer. With manifestation gifts, there is no relation. With ministry gifts, there generally is.

Ministry gifts are those gifts that ultimately determine where we fit in the body of Christ. The body of Christ works best when those whom God has placed within it are doing what He called and gifted them to do. That's why it's so important for people to discover their spiritual gifts, not only for their own fulfillment, but also to advance the work of God.

The Bible lists ministry gifts in three places: Romans 12:6-8, Ephesians 4:11 and 1 Peter 4:9-11. They are listed (and categorized) as follows:

1. *Equipping ministry gifts.* These are gifts for those whose task is to prepare others for ministry at all levels, from salvation to basic discipling (as in this course) to more advanced ministry training.
   a. *Apostle.* This can be otherwise translated as *emissary*, one who represents God to people in *new territory* for the gospel, in both preaching and leadership.
   b. *Prophet.* An individual who speaks forth for God on issues past, present and future, one who applies the Word of God in a supernatural way to the present situation. This also appears as a manifestation gift, but illustrates the difference between the two. As a manifestation gift, prophecy appears temporarily to an individual. An individual who is prophetic as a ministry gift does so on an ongoing basis.
   c. *Evangelist.* Someone who brings others to a saving knowledge of Jesus Christ as a special calling. This calling can be in the form of *mass evangelism* (to many people at once) or *personal evangelism* (to a few people at a time.)
   d. *Pastor-teacher.* One who both leads a congregation and imparts the Word to his or her flock. Jesus in His earthly ministry taught and led His disciples by both what He taught and what He did, and this is the model for those who would lead the church.
2. *Body ministry gifts.* These are the gifts which build up the body of Christ to do the work God called it to do.
   a. *Exhorter.* One who encourages and inspires others to keep going in Christ.
   b. *Teacher.* An individual who shows others what is in the Word of God and how it applies to their life situations. Unlike a pastor-teacher, a leadership role is not necessarily attached to this gift.
   c. *Service (or helps).* Those who have this gift are able to perform the necessary tasks that keep the church running on a routine basis. This is a special gift to

joyfully and effectively serve others in ways that, although not as visible as others, can reach people and win them to Christ.

d. *Administration.* These people handle the paperwork and usually the finances of the church. Some confuse this with leadership, but the two are not the same. Leadership is necessary to take the church forward. Administration is necessary to keep the day-to-day business of the church from strangling the church's forward momentum.

e. *Benevolence, or mercy.* People gifted in this way are able to dispense the material goods of the church to those in need in an effective way. Effective ministry of this type combines compassion with wisdom. This is a special ability to show sympathy to suffering people inside and outside the church. It can be exercised either in outreach ministry (such as visitation) or fulfilling material needs (food distribution, etc.).

f. *Giving.* A special gift, both in desire and ability, to meet the needs of God's work through financial generosity.

Determining Your Spiritual Gifts

Learning about your own spiritual gifts will help you understand how and where you fit into the body of Christ, help you set priorities for service, and give you direction for developing a personal ministry.

Spiritual gifts are a blessing. Therefore, the exercise of your gifts will necessarily bring enjoyment, fulfillment, and produce fruit. If your service doesn't, you probably are not serving in the right area.

Determining what one's spiritual gifts are is more than just picking what you feel your gift is out of the lists above. You may be missing hidden gifts! In the appendix to this lesson, we present the "Self-Discovery Survey" by Dr. Mike Chapman, pastor of City Church of God in Chattanooga, Tennessee, which will help you determine what your spiritual gifts are and where you are gifted to serve in the body of Christ.

A Final Reflection

Imagine that you have given your best friend a gift for his or her birthday. The big day arrives, and you call to find out how your gift was received. To your surprise, the reply comes, "Oh, I don't know, I haven't opened it yet. I decided to keep it wrapped up." Encouraging your friend to open it, you wait another day or two and call again, this time to ask if your gift was being put to good use. Instead, you hear these discouraging words: "Oh, I opened it all right, but decided to leave it in the closet."

God doesn't give spiritual gifts merely to have them left undiscovered or unused. Just as He has given you eyes, ears, and feet to be used in your physical body, so too He has given you gifts to be employed in the spiritual body, His church. In which areas of ministry has God gifted you? Is your local church profiting from the use of those gifts, or are your gifts still unwrapped and unused?

APPENDIX: SPIRITUAL GIFTS SELF-DISCOVERY SURVEY

Discovering Your Spiritual Gifts

Discover Your Grace Gift(s)

A Self-Discovery Survey

Dr. Mike Chapman
City Church of God
Chattanooga, Tennessee

Discover Your Grace Gifts
A Self-Discovery Survey

This survey is designed to help Christians discern their grace gift. It is not a fool-proof method; however, it should provide a guideline to help you discover your gift. For some who take this survey, your spiritual gift will become obvious. For others, it will help to narrow down your gift to two or three of the most likely possibilities. By using additional input, you should be able to further discern your spiritual gift.

Very little value will be derived from using this survey unless it is accompanied with studying the Biblical teachings on spiritual gifts. This survey is developed to be used as one part of a total study on spiritual gifts.

Survey Instructions

1. Write your response to each statement on the answer sheet.
2. Please respond to every statement. Do not leave any statement blank.
3. Respond to each statement by placing one of the following numbers in the appropriate box:
   2 = If the statement always or almost always characterizes you
   1 = If the statement sometimes characterizes you
   0 = If the statement rarely characterizes you

Scoring Instructions

1. After you have completed the survey, add the total of each column (A through G) and write this number on the appropriate line at the bottom of the column. This is your raw score.
2. Enter each raw score under the appropriate column on the Gift Graph.
3. Using the Conversion of Raw Score to Percentile Score table, determine your percentile score. Enter your percentile score on the graph. (For example: A raw score of 23 would convert to a percentile score of 77.)
4. Plot the percentile scores on the graph and draw a line between the dots.

Spiritual Gift Survey

2 = always 1 = sometimes 0 = rarely

1. I have a strong hatred for sin and grieve when I see it in my life or in the lives of other people.
2. I like to work on short-term rather than long-term projects.
3. I check out the facts carefully before I believe what I hear.
4. I enjoy counseling people.
5. I have the ability to make wise purchases and investments.
6. I have the ability to see the overall picture and clarify the long-range goals.
7. I am an extremely loving and kind person.
8. I speak frankly and boldly to a person when I sense a spiritual lack in his/her life.
9. I have the ability to recall the specific likes and dislikes of people.
10. I really get upset when someone uses a scripture out of context.
11. I enjoy talking to troubled, discouraged people to encourage them to live victoriously.
12. I like to give anonymously.
13. I enjoy delegating tasks and supervising people.
14. I quickly sense when a person is troubled about something.
15. I have the ability to discern the character and motives of people.
16. I am alert to detect and meet practical needs.
17. I am more interested in facts than opinions.
18. I believe that all teaching must have some practical application.
19. I like to feel a part of the ministries to which I contribute.
20. I like to accomplish tasks as quickly and efficiently as possible.
21. I am drawn to hurting people.
22. I set very high standards for myself because I desire to live strictly by Biblical standards.
23. I like to keep things in meticulous order.
24. I love to study and do research.
25. I see people's problems as stepping stones to victory in their lives.
26. I do not respond to emotional appeals. I give only as led by the Holy Spirit.
27. I have an awareness of resources available to complete a task.

Spiritual Gift Survey

2 = always 1 = sometimes 0 = rarely

28 I have a desire to remove hurts and bring healing to others.
29. I am very frank and outspoken; I usually do not mince words.
30. I would rather be a helper than a leader.
31. I like to present truth in a logical, systematic way.
32. I have a very positive mental attitude. I am an optimist.
33. I am a good financial manager.
34. I like clear lines of authority and responsibility.
35. I use firmness with people only as a last resort.
36. I have a deep concern for the reputation and program of God.
37. I have the desire to sense sincere appreciation and the ability to detect insincerity.
38. When teaching, I emphasize the accuracy of the point I am making more than how people can apply the truth to their lives.
39. I really like working with people.
40. I love to give freely of my money, time and talents.
41. I consider myself a visionary person.
42. I have a sensitivity to words and actions that hurt other people.
43. I want others to point out the blind spots in my life.
44. I am happiest when doing something helpful for someone.
45. I particularly enjoy doing word studies.
46. I easily accept people as they are without judging them.
47. I enjoy meeting needs without the pressure of appeals.
48. I am the happiest when working toward the accomplishment of specific goals.
49. I always look for the good in other people.
50. I have very strong opinions on most subjects and almost always verbalize them.
51. I love to entertain people in my home.
52. I like following established sources of truth.
53. I enjoy working with people who are eager to follow steps of action.
54. I am definitely not gullible.
55. I am more task-oriented than people-oriented.

Spiritual Gift Survey

2 = always 1 = sometimes 0 = rarely

56. I easily sense the spiritual or emotional mood of a person or group.
57. I feel a strong call to intercessory prayer.
58. I get frustrated when limitations of time are placed on a project.
59. I feel Bible study is foundational to all the gifts.
60. When someone has a problem, I love to give specific steps of action that will help move him out of the trial.
61. I am hard-working and usually successful at what I do.
62. I am very enthusiastic about whatever I am involved in.
63. I think it is very important to be sensitive to people's feelings.
64. To me, people and situations are either in the will of God or out of the will of God—there is no in between.
65. I tend to do more than I am asked to do.
66. I check out the knowledge source of other teachers.
67. When I have a problem in a relationship, I go to the other person right away to straighten it out.
68. I give high-quality gifts.
69. I really like to organize events and projects.
70. I often find myself serving as a mediator between people with troubled or broken relationships.
71. I would rather give a speech (sermon, lesson, lectures, etc.) than do the research for the speech.
72. I am energetic with a high energy level.
73. I am slow in accepting the viewpoint of others.
74. I like to think out loud when trying to analyze something.
75. I strongly believe that everything belongs to God, and I am just a channel.
76. I can endure criticism in order to get the job done.
77. I do not cope well with conflict or confrontation.
78. I would rather speak before a large group than to an individual.
79. I would rather do a job myself than delegate it to others.
80. I would rather help people by teaching a class than by personal counseling.
81. I can form my ideas better when I dialogue with someone rather than just analyzing things myself.

Spiritual Gift Survey

2 = always 1 = sometimes 0 = rarely

82. I enjoy giving what meets the practical needs of others.
83. I get great fulfillment in seeing pieces fit together and others enjoying the finished product.
84. I seem to have an inner instinct about things.
85. I enjoy research primarily to clarify and prove what I have presented.
86. I tend to be a perfectionist.
87. I would rather teach a class than be involved with personal witnessing.
88. I am a good verbal communicator.
89. I view hospitality as an opportunity to give.
90. I desire to move on to a new challenge when a previous one is completed.
91. I am ruled more by my heart than by my head.
92. When speaking before a group, I feel it is important to see an immediate response of commitment.
93. I would rather help someone by meeting a specific need than by teaching him how to provide for himself.
94. Reading is one of my hobbies.
95. I become frustrated when someone teaches without clear practical application.
96. I would rather function supportively in the background than speak in front of a group.
97. I like to plan ahead rather than take things as they come.
98. It is more important to me that everyone is happy rather than everything is exactly right.
99. I would rather spend time in prayer and fasting than organizing a Christian project.
100. I find it hard to say no when asked to help with a project.
101. When faced with a problem, I start by looking at God's Word.
102. I like to read how-to books.
103. I quickly volunteer to help when I see a need.
104. I really enjoy designing steps that help solve a problem.
105. Sometimes it is difficult for me to be decisive.

Conversion of Raw Score to Percentile Score

Raw Score	1	2	3	4	5	6	7	8	9	10	11	12	13	14	15
Percentile	3	7	10	13	17	20	23	27	30	33	37	40	43	47	50
Raw Score	16	17	18	19	20	21	22	23	24	25	26	27	28	29	30
Percentile	53	57	60	63	67	70	73	77	80	83	87	90	93	97	100

Gift Graph

	A Perceiver	B Server	C Teacher	D Exhorter	E Giver	F Adminis-trator	G Mercy Show-er
Raw Score							
Percentile							
100	•	•	•	•	•	•	•
95	•	•	•	•	•	•	•
90	•	•	•	•	•	•	•
85	•	•	•	•	•	•	•
80	•	•	•	•	•	•	•
75	•	•	•	•	•	•	•
70	•	•	•	•	•	•	•
65	•	•	•	•	•	•	•
60	•	•	•	•	•	•	•
55	•	•	•	•	•	•	•
50	•	•	•	•	•	•	•
45	•	•	•	•	•	•	•
40	•	•	•	•	•	•	•
35	•	•	•	•	•	•	•
30	•	•	•	•	•	•	•
25	•	•	•	•	•	•	•
20	•	•	•	•	•	•	•
15	•	•	•	•	•	•	•
10	•	•	•	•	•	•	•
5	•	•	•	•	•	•	•

Answer Sheet

2 = always 1 = sometimes 0 = rarely

	A	B	C	D	E	F	G
	1	2	3	4	5	6	7
	8	9	10	11	12	13	14
	15	16	17	18	19	20	21
	22	23	24	25	26	27	28
	29	30	31	32	33	34	35
	36	37	38	39	40	41	42
	43	44	45	46	47	48	49
	50	51	52	53	54	55	56
	57	58	59	60	61	62	63
	64	65	66	67	68	69	70
	71	72	73	74	75	76	77
	78	79	80	81	82	83	84
	85	86	87	88	89	90	91
	92	93	94	95	96	97	98
	99	100	101	102	103	104	105
Raw Score Total	A	B	C	D	E	F	G

Lesson 12: How to Have a Personal Ministry

(Subjects: Service, Good Works)

> *It is high time that the ideal of success should be replaced by the ideal of service* (Albert Einstein).
>
> *It is extraordinary how extraordinary the ordinary person is* (*Unknown*).

Memory Verse for This Lesson

> *For we are God's workmanship, created in Christ Jesus to do good works, which God prepared in advance for us to do* (Ephesians 2:10).

The Case for a Personal Ministry

Most of the great heroes of the Bible kept their day jobs.

- Adam the gardener
- Abraham the rancher
- David the shepherd and king
- Gideon the wheat farmer
- Jacob the herdsman
- Joseph the government official
- Luke the doctor
- Moses the legislator
- Nehemiah the statesman
- Noah the zoologist
- Paul the tent maker
- Peter the fisherman

They were laymen called by God to have a personal ministry.
God has not created two classes of Christians: occupational Christians who are the *ministers* and lay Christians who are the *ministry.* Instead, all Christians are ministers and the Great Commission is the ministry—reaching sinners, building believers, and nurturing the needy.

The Bible teaches the priesthood of all believers. "But you are a chosen people, a royal priesthood, a holy nation, a people belonging to God, that you may declare the praises of him who called you out of darkness into his wonderful light" (1 Peter 2:9).

God's plan is for every Christian to have a personal ministry. "For we are God's workmanship, created in Christ Jesus to do good works, which God prepared in advance for us to do" (Ephesians 2:10).

What motivates some men to have a dynamic personal ministry? And perhaps more to the point, what can motivate you to serve Christ in a meaningful way?

We are motivated to personal ministry when we come to fully recognize the incredible gift God has given us in Christ Jesus His Son. When we know Him more intimately we inevitably want to do something to please Him. Why? Because when we learn how deeply and radically His grace, mercy, and kindness have touched and healed us, we are filled with a deep sense of gratitude.

We can't help but want to do a work of service to show our thanks. The only reason we may not yet long to serve Him is that we do not yet fully understand the riches that are ours in Christ Jesus.

The Relationship Between Faith and Works

The relationship between faith and works (service, personal ministry) has long been a source of confusion. The issue: How is a man saved—by faith, works, or some combination of the two? From the following verses, see if you can settle the issue once and for all in your own mind. It is critical to the believer's freedom that he understand whether or not his good works are a *component* of his salvation or a *by-product* of his salvation.

According to Ephesians 2:8, 9, what part does performing good works (service) play in our becoming Christians?

Though good works play no part in *becoming* a Christian, what part do they play in demonstrating that we are Christians? See James 2:14, 17, 26.

Christians typically make one of two mistakes when considering faith and works:

1. They believe their salvation is dependent upon their works. They may serve from a sense of fear or compulsive duty.
2. When Christians do perform good deeds, they may unwittingly think their good deeds somehow qualify them for salvation.

However, as the English apologist John Jewel points out, faith and works go together:

> *Besides, though we say we have no meed [reward] at all by our own works and deeds, but appoint all the means of our salvation to be in Christ alone, yet say we not that for this cause men ought to live loosely and dissolutely; nor that it is enough for a Christian to be baptized only and to believe; as though there were nothing else required at his hand. For true faith is lively and can in no wise be idle. Thus therefore teach we the people that God hath called us, not to follow riot and wantonness, but, as Paul saith, "unto good works to walk in them"; that God hath plucked us out "from the power of darkness, to serve the living God," to cut away all the remnants of sin, and "to work our salvation in fear and trembling"; that it may appear how that the Spirit of sanctification is in our bodies and that Christ himself doth dwell in our hearts.*[1]

When we are saved, Jesus Christ comes into our lives and into our hearts and makes us new people, something we cannot take credit for because we did not have the resources to accomplish this. Once God dwells in us, though, the Holy Spirit, through His works of sanctification and the baptism in the Holy Spirit, compels and equips us to do the works that He has called us to do. In this way both faith and works have the same ultimate source, which is God himself.

Have you settled the issue of how you have been saved? In your own words write down the reason you believe you have received salvation:

If for any reason you are unsure of your salvation, don't despair. It is not God's desire that any should be lost (Matthew 18:14; 2 Peter 3:9). Review Lesson 1 and see if you can settle the issue through the material presented. If not, discuss your thoughts, concerns, and feelings with your discipler. You can know for sure: "God, who has called you into fellowship with His Son Jesus Christ, is faithful" (1 Corinthians 1:9).

The Call to Serve

Read Ephesians 2:10:

- For what purpose have we been created?

- Who decides what good works we will do?

Scripture tells us that we have been created for the express purpose of performing good works. God himself has preordained some special form of personal ministry for you. This personal ministry is not something you watch someone else do, but service that you yourself perform with the empowerment of the Holy Spirit.

As covered in Lesson 11, every believer has at least one spiritual gift. This gift forms the basis for our service. According to 1 Peter 4:10, how are we to employ our gifts?

From 1 Peter 4:11, how are we to speak for God?

How are we to serve Him?

We are all members of the body of Christ, which is the church. We are called to serve. We use our spiritual gifts to perform our service.

From the following verses write down three reasons we serve:

Ephesians 4:12b

____

Ephesians 4:13

____

1 Peter 4:11b

____

Six Areas of Personal Ministry

You may be wondering, *But what can I do?* You can do a lot. There are six areas of personal ministry in which anyone with a sincere desire to serve God can help, whether trained or not. These include at home, in the church, in the community, across economic and cultural barriers, at work, and to the world. Let's briefly explore each area.

1. Ministry in the Family

A personal ministry to our family is the most important service we can ever do. If you really desire to have a powerful ministry, then disciple your family.

If you are like many men, you may have been devoting little time to the spiritual nourishment of your family. Whether this is the case for you or not, you should develop a specific plan to minister to your family.

Most men are leaving a trail of broken relationships strewn along the path of their personal ambition. Children sit in psychiatric offices angry to tears. Why? Because their dads are too busy to spend any time with them. As one troubled young boy said, "Can't do nothin' without a dad."

We don't want to win the world but lose our family in the process. No amount of success at the office can compensate for failure at home.

What can you do? Try having a time of family devotions, perhaps in the morning before school and work. Keep it to 5 to 15 minutes and close in prayer. Shoot for three or four days a week. You can begin with an example from everyday life and then read a related Bible passage. Some days you may want to read something prepared by others. Close in prayer. Children tend to pray for themselves, so pick someone who is hurting or in need to pray for each day to get their eyes off themselves.

Activities that get your children involved in spiritual things (either with you or on their own) will produce huge dividends. Always pray before meals. Force your children to attend church the same way you force them to attend school.

2. Ministry in the Church

The church is the bride of Christ, and was instituted by God to function as a body. Your spiritual gifts can surely be put to use in your church, especially if your church emphasizes the priesthood of all believers.

Gifts of service can be employed in a personal ministry of helping others. Gifts of teaching can be employed in a personal ministry of teaching adult Sunday school, children's programs, or a midweek home Bible study. Gifts of mercy can be directed to hurting people in the church body.

Perhaps the greatest service we can render to the local church is through personal evangelism, as we discussed in Lesson 10. One way to make this easier is through a small group, team effort. One such program is Covenant Group Evangelism and Team Ministry. The appendix at the end of this lesson gives an overview of this ministry.

3. Ministry in the Community

If you are out in the marketplace on a regular basis, God may give you a desire to minister in the community. *How*?, you wonder.

God may lead you to make a commitment to one of three areas—the education system, politics, or civic affairs. The single greatest reason that society and culture is in such disarray is that committed disciples of Christ have not been salt and light where it counts. When we separate our faith from our public life we err. Tremendous opportunities for personal ministry in the community exist because of the leadership vacuum left by Christians unwilling to be counted for Christ in public. How about you?

Examples: Campaign for a Christian candidate, run for office, serve on the school board or PTA, become an active member of the Chamber of Commerce or a service club, sponsor an evangelistic breakfast (such as the Resurrection Breakfast) or luncheon.

4. Ministry Across Economic and Cultural Barriers

A trip to Africa or Haiti will certainly open your eyes to the poverty around the world. Yet, in every community we drive by shanties just as impoverished as any Third-World country. In every community a host of ministries are directed to break the yoke of poverty and need among the downtrodden.

There are youth ministries for disadvantaged youth, drug ministries for addicts, pregnancy counseling centers for the unwed mothers, feeding stations for the hungry, and housing for the homeless.

Consider reaching beyond the comfort of your own culture into the bowels of your community. A personal ministry serving alongside an existing ministry organization may be exactly right for you.

5. Ministry at Work

A fertile field for a personal ministry is at work. First and foremost, you can have a vital ministry at work through witnessing for Christ by your character, actions, and words. We each have the responsibility to share our faith with others. Work provides us with a rich pool of relationships among broken, hurting people who need to hear God's message of love, hope, and forgiveness.

Most opportunities to have a personal ministry at work will come simply through your everyday relationships—if you take the initiative. More structured ministry opportunities include a luncheon Bible study, inviting a colleague to a Bible study or outreach event, ministry to associates who are hurting, inviting peers to worship in your church.

6. Ministry to the World

The Great Commission includes making disciples "to the uttermost part of the world." We are called to bring the gospel to the whole world. How can we be part of the Great Commission?

Most of us can contribute some financial support to ministries reaching out across the world. You can help your vision grow by inviting visiting missionaries to stay in your home. Everyone can pray for missionaries. Perhaps you could have a ministry of encouragement by writing to missionaries on a regular basis. Everyone would benefit from taking a missions trip, especially among the poor. An excellent vehicle for this is Matthew 25 Men; more informtion on this can be obtained from Lay Ministries International. Certainly not everyone is able to go, but if you can go, you will never be the same again.

Christian Versus Secular Service

Should Christians work on secular projects? Non-Christians prefer to work on projects not identified as distinctly Christian; Christians on the other hand acknowledge that everything belongs to God. "For everything in heaven and earth is yours" (1 Chronicles 29:11). Therefore, all noble projects are spiritual. All good deeds are spiritual. Said differently, no project God calls the Christian to do is secular.

There are two kinds of fruit the Christian will produce—one that lasts and one that doesn't. We are to be *ambassadors* for the kingdom of God (producing lasting fruit) and *stewards* of creation (which will pass away). The highest goal of the humanist is to leave the world a better place. This, too, is a fruit of Christian service, but it must be kept in perspective.

Our stewardship of culture and society is a means to an end; it must never be confused with fruit that lasts. "The elements will be destroyed by fire, and the earth and everything in it will be laid bare" (2 Peter 3:10). Only God and people who turn to Christ live forever—that is lasting fruit. So always keep that end in view.

Christians are a special interest group, and the Great Commission is the special interest; it should receive a special emphasis. Jesus handpicked us to do good works that will last. "You did not choose me, but I chose you to go and bear fruit—fruit that will last" (John 15:16). We will receive no help from non-Christians to produce fruit that will last, so we alone must do it.

Steps to Becoming Involved

The abundant Christian life is the overflow of knowing, loving, and serving Jesus Christ. Hopefully this lesson has sparked some new ideas for your own personal ministry if you don't already have one. Let's review some practical steps you should take to get going:

1. *Spiritual Gifts*: Determine your spiritual gifts (See Lesson 11).
2. *The Church Body:* Explore ministry possibilities within the church body where God has placed you.
3. *Family*: Explore ministry needs/opportunities within your own family.
4. *Other Areas*: Review the other areas discussed above for possible outlets of personal ministry.
5. *Seek Counsel*: Seek the counsel of your pastor and spiritually mature friends.
6. *Daily Opportunities*: Consider that opportunities for service that present themselves during the normal course of daily living are divinely appointed, not merely interruptions.
7. *Set Priorities*: You cannot do everything, so set priorities and stick to them.
8. *Experiment*: Finally, reflect on the ways you have served, are serving, or feel led to serve the Lord. In the space provided write down several new personal ministry possibilities:

- ____
- ____
- ____
- ____
- ____

Begin to pray and experiment with each of these possibilities. As you step into the water in faith, God will reveal His plan for you—good works He prepared in advance for you to do.

Appendix: Convenant Group Evangelism and Team Ministry

Local church evangelism teaching, training and outreach in a small group concept

1. Our major challenge: *sustainability*
    - The *most difficult thing* to accomplish regarding an evangelism program in a local church is *keeping the ministry active and growing* once the initial launch has been completed.
    - Historically we have tended to be *event-oriented* with evangelism (such as a weekend meeting of teaching and training) rather than *purpose-driven.*
    - *Events are not the ministry!* One big outreach, followed by a few visitation attempts does not result is sustaining the full ministry including follow-up, relationship building and individual discipleship.
2. The plan: *team ministry*
    - The *big* idea is organizing the laity into a *small group environment* with accountability to a group leader and to a pastor. This ensures that all of the evangelism

goals are accomplished including regular and ongoing visitation, prayer walking, community outreach, follow-up and discipleship.

- ⊙ The *basic plan* consists of initially *forming groups from the laity consisting of 10 to 12 members.* Each group would be *subdivided into four teams of three to four members each with a team leader over each one.* The goal would be to keep increasing the number of groups by recruiting group leaders and getting them to help recruit other participants.

3. The *four teams within each group* are as follows:

- ***Neighborhood prayer walk and intercessory prayer team***

  - ⊙ This team will, in advance of the home visitation team, prayer walk the neighborhood targeted by the group leader as well as involve themselves in regular, daily, focused intercessory prayer for the evangelism efforts of the covenant group.

  - ⊙ Some, because of physical limitations or other reasons, will remain at the church (or their home) and offer intercessory prayer for the teams as they go out.

- ***Church introduction team***

  - ⊙ This team consists of those who are willing to do visitation but are not yet comfortable presenting the gospel in the home. These individuals would visit homes with the intent of introducing the church, inviting people to the services, leaving literature (tracts and church brochure) and inquiring of and offering prayer for any need. They would cover a large number of homes in the community.

- ***Personal evangelism and follow-up team***
  - ⦿ This team will introduce the church and follow through with the actual presentation of the gospel. This team should be assigned specific homes for a two hour period. They usually do not get to more than three to four homes in an evening.
  - ⦿ Initially, follow-up begins with these teams members. As the prospect list grows we recommend that a separate follow-up effort be initiated. It is our intent to start Bible study in the homes of anyone receptive to the gospel message, not just those who make a profession of Christ.
- ***Servant evangelism team***
  - ⦿ Servant evangelism projects are designed to "show God's love in practical ways with no strings attached." Essentially, servant evangelism is accomplished by any activity that is done in the name of Jesus and provides a beneficial service to people in a setting where no financial consideration is expected or accepted (not even donations).
  - ⦿ Servant evangelism softens the hearts of persons who are not yet Christians—people who often think the church exists only for itself or that it only wants people's time and money. By doing a low-risk activity that shows high grace, those resistant to the faith may (now or in the future) become more open to the saving message of Jesus Christ.

4. The Covenant Evangelism Groups and Subteams
   - ***The particulars***